The Smallest Things

The Smallest Things

On the enduring power of family

Nick Duerden

A memoir of tiny dramas

Elliott&Thompson

First published 2019 by
Elliott and Thompson Limited
27 John Street, London WC1N 2BX
www.eandtbooks.com

ISBN: 978-1-78396-415-4

9 8 7 6 5 4 3 2 1

A catalogue record for this book is available from the British
Library.

Typesetting by Marie Doherty
Printed in the UK by TJ International Ltd

For my grandparents,
and in memory of my mother

'You know, the withering of the family tree is one of the saddest things ever.'

Old Filth, Jane Gardam

one

The memories I have of my grandparents are just snapshots, really, fragmented and disjointed, incomplete. For all my life, and at least half of theirs, we have lived at a distance of 597 easyJet miles from one another, me in London, them in an industrial suburb of Milan. We saw each other infrequently, and, due to my grandfather's reluctance to leave both his home turf and the local bowls club, they rarely made the journey over here. I can remember them visiting only the once, shortly after my parents had separated and we had left the vertiginous council block for the newbuild council house that we were excited by but with which my grandfather remained largely unimpressed. So we went to them, summer holidays mostly, ten days a year, two weeks at most. They spoke not a word of English – 'Gatwick' they pronounced 'Getvich' – and my Italian was, and remains, pidgin at best. Consequently, I have never had a proper conversation with either of them, no eloquent heart-to-heart, no outpouring of feelings, with much over our years together left so frustratingly unsaid.

By the time I reached eighteen, I was no longer required to endure interminable family holidays. Italy is a beautiful country, it's true, but the industrial suburbs of Milan in stifling August heat is something few people need to experience more than once. As an adult, my chunks of time with them consequently slimmed to long weekends a couple of times a year, occasionally with a girl-friend, then my wife, then my wife and children, but never the dog. At first I suffered these weekends dutifully because I was young and brash, and because time in Milan stood so tauntingly still and I didn't. But as I aged and slowed, and as they did too, these trips out of normal life became visits to cherish, to burn into my mind's eye for the time when the inevitable happened and they weren't around any more.

I became more acutely aware of this inalienable fact when they were in their seventies, and I in my twenties. They had had their three score years and ten, and so biblically at least (my grandparents were mildly observant Catholics, and never missed a televised sermon by the Pope) they believed they were on borrowed time. Though the weekend visits maintained their time-honoured non-event status – we would go nowhere, do nothing, simply spend companionable hours together around the dinner table, in front of the television, playing games of cards – the farewells became increasingly resonant, containing levels of emotional drama that would be proud to grace a Nicholas Sparks novel. Tears would pool in their eyes as I shouldered my overnight bag and kissed them goodbye. Neither of us said that we might never see one another again, that this was it, because we didn't need to. The unspoken is sometimes louder than what's said.

But then there they were again the next year, and the next year after that. And then a decade went by, and it was clear they were going nowhere. I started to ponder on the many wonders of the Mediterranean diet, and an increasing evidence of the sustaining powers of a largely sedentary life.

Time with my grandparents really did operate at a more gradual pace. It was a stagnant thing, swollen with inactivity, no pressing need to maintain the urgent thrust of modern life because here life wasn't modern at all. It had stopped with my grandfather's retirement years earlier, and these days tock only followed tick if tock could be bothered. There were no distractions, little incident, no pressing places to be, nothing to get done. No Wi-Fi. Almost every element of them and their small, spotlessly clean flat was, to me, preserved in aspic: the same ancient cooker that required you to stoop to light the gas in the same unmodernised kitchen; the same circular dining-room table; the mantelpiece clock, its curves reminiscent of a Fiat 500, chiming sonorously on the half hour as if half hours were worth marking; the creak in the living-room floorboards; the wrought-iron chandelier in the hallway.

No shoes were allowed on the polished floors of the flat, and upon entry I was required to relinquish mine and accommodate myself inside a pair of my grandfather's slippers. Choosing never to wear these, to slide instead across the floor in nothing but a dangerous pair of socks, represented a low-level rebellion that never failed to thrill me. In their presence, I was somehow forever the child.

Be careful, my grandmother would chide, as I slid from living room to bathroom and back again without lifting my feet. *You could fall over.*

I never fell over.

At home in London, I found myself constantly impatient for novelty. I grew bored easily and relaxed reluctantly. But in Milan, I liked how their home remained unchanged, that whatever else might be happening in my own life, and the speed at which I lived it, from relationship to breakup to new relationship, from studio flat to one-bedroom, from two bedrooms to a house, from no children to children, everything here was as it always was. There were rituals here I carefully preserved – in pursuit, perhaps, of living nostalgia. For example, I always placed a hot thumb on the wall-mounted barometer in the bathroom to watch the mercury rise towards 30° because that was what I had always done; or the way I would unfailingly disturb the intricate lace doilies draped on top of the burnt-orange living-room sofa in pursuit of chi-chi decoration, whenever I sat down to read. Every morning I would choose the same fake china cup from which to drink my milky coffee, the one with its now-faded image of a just-engaged Charles and Diana on the side, her smile ambiguous even then.

And I loved how my grandparents never changed either, their quirks and characters already long established but more deeply entombed into what it was that made them and kept them upright, the two oldest people in my life, this mysterious couple with whom I could never fully communicate, and whose relationship with their daughter, my mother, was always so strained, often to breaking point, but towards whom I could only ever feel unconditional love because that's how their own love for me was so palpably expressed.

It was an understated emotion, though, perhaps typically for people of their generation, dispensed with a fussy anxiety by her and a taciturn masculinity by him. In insisting I sit at the kitchen table within minutes of my arrival each year so that she could boil me an egg and present it in the same old egg cup, my grandmother was demonstrating that she still thought of me as the eleven-year-old who, one summer's day, perhaps out of nothing else to say, announced that boiled eggs were his favourite food. To her, I would always be her eleven-year-old grandson. In his firm handshake, and the occasional soft shoulder charge, my grandfather, a man of few words, let it be known that I was his family.

They would always impart advice, tips, offering up their expertise and purported wisdom on everything from food to fashion. My grandmother taught me things she thought I couldn't have possibly learned by myself because such knowledge could only ever emanate from the older generation, from *them*. Educating me in how to live was something they took very seriously.

Keenly aware that I was entering my teenage years fatherless, my grandfather's attempts to offer some paternal steerage may have been clumsy and awkward, but were filled with good intent. Under the Formica kitchen table was a tucked-away drawer which opened to reveal items that would be the envy of any man's toolbox. Here there were flat-head screwdrivers alongside claw hammers, crescent wrenches and vice grips, items the names and uses of which I would never learn. My grandfather was a handyman, someone who would roll up his sleeves, and make, and do. He could fix things. I was as interested in DIY as I was in the Cossack communities of eastern Luxembourg, but each year he would try nevertheless to coax me into helping him reattach the knob that had once again fallen off the ancient cooker, because this was how men bonded: in nuts and bolts and oil and smears. I never grew fond of oil smears.

I remember arriving one summer by myself. I was perhaps seventeen, eighteen, having just re-sat exams I had so disastrously failed the year before, and was wearing a new pair of 501s, tighter than my usual jeans perhaps, but no tighter than current fashion – then in the grip of Nick Kamen-spearheaded, mid-eighties mania – dictated. My grandfather cast his own deeply unsartorial eye over me before announcing to my grandmother that I was plainly dressing to the right when men should in fact dress to the left. I had scant idea how to explain to him, in my faltering Italian, that I didn't actually choose to dress to the right at all, it just happened to . . . *settle* there. And so I simply smiled, awkwardly, blushing, then swiftly directed him over to his tool drawer, and to safer territory. 'A claw hammer, you say?'

I remember, too, the impeccable rigmarole of lunch, how my grandmother had transformed slow cooking into an art form, not because she was precise but simply because, now long retired, her universe restricted accordingly, she had little else with which to occupy her days. A boiling saucepan of spaghetti, which by rights should take no longer than nine minutes to become appropriately al dente, she could make last an hour or more, driving my starving stomach to both distraction and the bread bin. Lunch, when it did finally arrive onto the table I had helped set an hour previously, was wonderful, better than any restaurant; the spaghetti preceded by slices of prosciutto and followed by a *secondo piatto* of chicken breast and fried potatoes, a side dish of freshly washed lettuce and ripe, warm beef tomatoes, with grapes and cake and coffee as dessert.

In the afternoons I would ride my grandfather's rickety post-war bicycle through the streets of Milan, chasing my own boredom on endless summer holidays, desperately trying to find the *Senso Unico* that so many street signs pointed towards before eventually being made aware that *Senso Unico* meant One Way. My grandmother would always feign admiration as I boasted how far I had cycled in a single afternoon, barely breaking a sweat.

And every day would end the way it always ended, the television providing a backdrop to the evening's entertainment. At any time of the day, on any day of the week, Italian TV provides a great many magazine programmes that last several hours, and feature cooking segments, phone-in quizzes, and high-kicking song-and-dance routines. My grandfather would browse these during dinner, keeping the remote control in his clutches and perhaps paying particular attention to the women who were habitually more attractive than their much older male counterparts, before summarily switching over to Rai Uno for the news. This he would watch for ten to fifteen minutes before abruptly switching over to Rete 4 for *Murder, She Wrote*. It didn't matter that we had missed the first quarter of an hour – and the murder itself – because they had probably seen this episode anyway. But just when I found myself getting into the plot he would reach again for the remote, now deciding he wanted to know the weather forecast for the following day, and after that would develop a renewed hunger for the variety shows, some of which had found a second wind and were now able to continue for several more hours yet. I'm not sure I ever found out whodunnit.

And then it was time for cards, the curtain call to every day here, a game called *Quindici*, which we would play, at a leisurely pace, for the remainder of the evening, my grandfather keeping at least one eye on a Serie A football match. At approximately half past ten, eleven o'clock, we would wind up, and as he and I cleared the table, my grandmother would pull out the foldout bed from the wall unit, narrow and firm and with the same freshly laundered and crisply ironed sheets I had slept beneath for years.

'Buona notte,' they would tell me, at length. *Good night.*

As they pottered slowly in the kitchen, and then in the bathroom, I would wait impatiently in bed, intent on staying awake. Angela Lansbury was all well and good, card games too, but by eleven o'clock

14

at night I had other preoccupations to attend to, and once they were safely in their room, door closed, lights out, I'd begin to click through the multiple Italian cable TV channels, the volume low, in fervent and necessary search of a programme that would reward my protracted days here with something illicit, and exciting, and rude.

How to prepare lunch

*G*ood *food cannot be rushed. Take your time.*

For spaghetti al pesto, set a large saucepan of well-salted water to boil on the lowest possible gas setting. This way, your saucepan will never burn. Allow 30–45 minutes. If in the fridge you have the rind of Parmesan cheese – and it will be entirely likely that you do, tucked into a corner for just such an occasion – then drop this gently into the water for flavour.

Do not guess the correct amount of spaghetti for four people, and do not consult the packaging. Never trust the instructions on the side of food packaging. Instead, weigh the pasta on a set of scales, and make your own mental calculations, a process that can take upwards of several minutes.

Prepare the salad, setting the lettuce in a colander in the sink and washing thoroughly. Let the water continue to flow irrespective of the waste. Wash two or three beef tomatoes, and cut into generous thumbnail-moon slices. Place in salad bowl, sprinkle with salt and a generous splash of olive oil. For quantity of oil, think: children's paddling pool. Add vinegar. Mix thoroughly for no less than 15 minutes.

Check the saucepan on the gas, which should at last be approaching a very slight simmer. Add the pasta. Leave for 25 minutes.

From the fridge, retrieve yesterday's leftover meat. Place frying pan onto the cooker on the lowest possible gas setting, add olive oil. Prepare meat with salt and sea-soning. When the times comes – not yet, later; patience – lightly fry.

Request help to set the table, first clearing it of its sundry items – reading glasses, crossword puzzle maga-zines, pencil stubs, the vase of plastic flowers – then cover it with the tablecloth. If there are guests, among them grandchildren (even grandchildren in their forties), place a plastic sheet beneath the tablecloth for likely spillages. Set the table with knives, forks, spoons, placemats for plates, coasters for glasses. The thick cotton napkin with its own napkin ring is his, the one with the knot is hers. Guests can choose from those clean and recently ironed in the drawer. A bottle of fizzy water, a bottle of red wine. Assorted packets of breadsticks. Some ham, crudo and cotto, a few slices of salami Milano. The bread bag with at least four white bread rolls in them. It is permissible to use the fresh bread rolls bought first thing this morning, but do try to use the ones frozen the night before. These should have been placed on the windowsill during the preparation of lunch, where they will have enjoyed generous sunlight for thawing; otherwise put directly onto a gas hob, the gas on the lowest possible setting. The bread will not burn but will merely have its tummy tickled towards appropriate warmth and digestibility.

Taste pasta. If ready, give another 10 minutes, add more salt. Plate, then drench liberally with pesto sauce.

Serve.

. . . .

two

Given how little time I spent with them over the years, it seems strange to me how vivid the memories remain. But then our grandparents help create, unwittingly or otherwise, some of our more treasured memories in life. Mine centre mostly around those stultifying summer holiday visits, when heat always makes people act strangely. I can still see the windows flung open during long evenings, inviting in any breeze that might have been passing, my grandmother insisting I drink water because dehydration was a predatory danger and one to be avoided – on her watch, at least – at any cost. Nights in Milan could last forever, the kind of too-hot summer nights that would deny sleep, bring lizards out onto the wall, and reveal in all of us short fuses. By mid morning, as if fuelled by the event that was breakfast (for my mother never ate as much as my grandparents wanted her to), tempers would fray, there would be raised voices and shouted accusations between them, the precise ingredients of which I never quite bothered to pick up on. It wasn't my business.

I never looked too closely behind the façade of my grandparents. That's who they were to me – a title, a role – and that was enough. Taking stock is something we tend only to do late in life, and now that at last I am, I realise just how much I took them for granted, how little they intrigued me at a time when they were perhaps the most intriguing people in my life. Regardless, I don't think I have ever felt quite so connected to people who have remained so ultimately unknowable to me. Fifty years have always separated us, and that half century divided us in every sense. We were completely different people, with different interests, appreciations and pursuits. Of course we were fated never to fully bond, or see eye to eye. My grandparents had lived through war, horror and hardship; I lived through the era of Adidas, computer games and the arrival of a fourth channel onto terrestrial TV. I could hardly compete, my life a litany of trivialities compared to theirs.

Their careers had been blue-collar, proper work, hard work and poorly paid. They rarely travelled outside Italy (to Yugoslavia annually, my grand-mother's place of birth; once or twice to England, to see us). They didn't read books, had little interest in art, in music. I once went to Milan for work, to interview an American rock band whose stock-in-trade was their raucous bad behaviour, frat boys who never really grew up and whose spectacular global success allowed them to remain puerile well into midlife. I flew out a couple of days earlier to spend time with my grandparents and, while watching TV on the tiny set that sat on top of the fridge, saw their latest video come on. I pointed it out, explaining that this was who I was here to speak to; they were staying in one of the city's grandest hotels. My grandfather, who was doing the crossword in the other room, came into the kitchen and gazed upon the TV screen impassively, slowly taking in the band's antics as they lip-synched to their hyperactive song, and then studied me with infinite disappointment in his eyes, unable to comprehend either how their music was worthy of comment by any sane human being, or quite why it was my job to report on it. *This* was how I chose to live my life?

Ultimately, he accepted the nebulous nature of my chosen profession in this curious new world in which he found himself a dweller, but it hardly helped bridge the gulf that remained. Yet the gulf between us ultimately didn't matter. He was my grandfather: I loved him, and him me. We all love our grandparents, even the complicated, crotchety ones.

But, reliably late in life, I wanted to understand the bond that continues to connect each of us to our own, and to begin to appreciate it more. I wanted to think about them, at length: what they have meant to me, and what I may have meant to them. Like all grandparents, mine were strange and secretive, the stories they had before I came along to hog the limelight only ever hinted at. I had been guilty of taking them for granted, but the more I came to think of their peripheral presence in my life, the more I realised it was simply this presence I valued most.

They were always there, and I never wanted them gone.

~

Throughout life, we can, and – if my poor track record is anything to go by – summarily do, drift apart from friends. As our circumstances change, we become disconnected from them, and lost from one another, not so umbilical after all. People we might have known intimately years previously can somehow become abrupt strangers with whom we now have precious little in common, save for the mutual awkwardness we feel whenever we do manage to meet. It happens to all of us; a regular, everyday occurrence. It is sad, I think, to realise that those we had once considered so close can go on to become so remote. But then this is what life does: it refocuses and resettles us. Perhaps that in part is why the internet is so popular: it reconnects us to those at the point at which we feel most alone, and vulnerable.

But many of us won't ever really drift apart from our grandparents in any comparable way. Our grandparents remain to us who they always were, even though they surely change just as radically as anybody else. But there they stay, ever reliable, forever reachable, their feelings towards us either undimmed or effectively masked: they love us, and accept us, still. They overlook our shortcomings, they forgive us our trespasses, and excuse the fact that we don't call, or write, as often as we should. Theirs is a role without a sell-by date, uninfluenced by whim or changing fortunes. They watch our waistlines fluctuate with concern rather than scorn. No one in my own life has ever exhibited a greater consideration for the state of my bowels than my grandmother. Every time I flushed, she sighed with relief.

They are always unfailingly happy to hear from us, even during those times when nobody else is. I would regularly fail to call mine anywhere near as often as I should have done during my twenties and thirties – I was travelling a lot for work, I was busy – but each time I did, they responded with such joy in their voices that I was humbled again by the love they continued so unconditionally to convey.

And I never did forget them, even if it might have seemed to them, from time to time, that I did. When I met a woman and fell in love with her, it was to them I wanted to show her off the most, the two of us arriving in Milan happy and excited that we had reached a stage in our relationship where we were doing this sort of thing – introducing one another to relatives, laying foundations – and also wanting them to know what I thought I already knew: that here was a woman I might stay with and, one day, marry. They delicately didn't point out that I had previously brought them *another* girlfriend with whom I had thought I was laying foundations, but were instead as graciously kind to my new one as they had been to the ex. The wisdom of old people is often a silent wisdom.

We were there for a week, my new girlfriend and I, and it was a memorable time, albeit mostly for the wrong reasons, because it once again showed up the gulf that can exist between us and them: a wholly different approach to the world and its impetuous possibilities. It also offered to me overwhelming proof that our grandparents really do change, even if we fail mostly to notice it. Because as our own worlds continue to expand, theirs contracts. It is in this diminishment that events can become chaotic, even catastrophic.

It had been a simple desire for an afternoon's drive that finally made me notice just how restricted my grandfather's world had become while I was busy looking elsewhere. This drive turned into a journey that took us almost all the way to Switzerland and, during what was surely a panic attack that prompted him to drive far too fast for far too long, to hell and back.

◦

It was a warm spring day in the north of Italy. I had suggested we all take a trip up to Lake Como, an hour away: my girlfriend, Elena, later my wife, had never been to Italy before, and I wanted to make good my promise to her that Italy was more beautiful than this bland suburb of Milan might suggest. My grandparents rarely left their bland suburb, however, but I was adamant that this would make a nice change for them. We could have lunch in a restaurant, our treat. It might be fun.

As I spoke this suggestion out loud, consternation etched across both their faces, and corrugated their brows. We had never previously been to a restaurant together, because why on earth would we? The cooker worked perfectly well, and the fridge had food in it. This had always been my grandmother's pervading logic, my grandmother who had grown up in the shadow of encroaching war and its lingering devastation afterwards. My grandfather's argument was that he didn't like to drive too far any more. He was, by now, in his mid eighties. He pointed out that if it was fun we were after, a new takeaway pizza place had just opened around the corner.

We pressed our case. I could drive, I told him, save him the bother. My grandfather nixed the idea as preposterous. In England, we drove on the left; in Italy, the right. I couldn't possibly cope with the reversal. So I countered: Elena could drive.

My girlfriend was Spanish. The Spanish drive on the right, too.

A delicate discussion such as this cannot take place in normal time. Press him too hard and too quickly, and he might be likely to explode. A certain stealth is required, and so stealth was what I employed. The back-and-forth continued, in fits and starts, over the next several days, interrupted by mealtimes, by crossword puzzles and whatever happened to be on the television at any time. I had mostly given up all hope, and suggested to Elena that we should just go to Como by ourselves; the train could take us. But then, shortly before we were due to return to London, my grandfather cleared his throat while his wife watched expectantly, and announced it might be nice for us all to take a drive up to Lake Como. We could have lunch in a restaurant, their treat.

I looked between my grandparents, their impassive faces at once giving away so little but also conveying just how much they must have discussed this earlier, while we were out, heated discussions no doubt, and, I'm guessing, much pleading on the part of my grandmother. In this moment, I loved them both so very dearly. That this conciliatory effort had cost them was not lost on me.

Elena and I grinned, then put on our shoes, ready to go. Then we waited while they readied themselves. After a while, we took our books out and began to read. My grandparents readying themselves for an hour's trip in the car involved a mandatory change of clothes, the quick but necessary ironing of a blouse for her, and a pair of good corduroy trousers for him. The application of jewellery, a nice scarf and a light jacket in case the balmy weather suddenly turned. Some perfume, a dab of eau de cologne.

At some point, my grandfather went downstairs to warm up the car – because you could never just simply turn on the engine and drive away, you had to sit in it for a good ten minutes while it percolated. My grandmother double-checked that all the windows on the third-floor flat were securely shut, that the gas was off, the fridge door definitely closed, the TV on standby and the neighbours alerted that we would be out for some time in case of emergency.

I looked at my watch. By this point we were already late for lunch.

'Andiamo,' she said at last. *Let's go.*

It had been some years, decades even, since they had last driven this route. Whenever I had travelled with them in the car previously, the journey had always been fraught. My grandfather didn't like a draught, so the windows, even in high summer, could only ever be opened a crack. Conversation had to be kept to a minimum: he was concentrating. The radio? There was no radio. My grandmother, up front alongside him, played navigator, Grace

Kelly-ish in her scarf and posture while he stooped over the steering wheel, absorbed in the task at hand.

They were much the same now, and so Elena and I sat meekly, childishly, in the back of the small car, knees to chins. The silence crackled with an anticipatory foreboding, for my grandfather seemed unusually tense today, clutching so hard at the wheel that I feared it might come loose. Out of his eyeline, my grandmother stretched her hand behind her seat and towards me, and suddenly I was swamped with déjà vu: a time years earlier, driving the six hours to Yugoslavia one August holiday, she had done this as well, signalling to me that he was stressed, and that we might be in peril. Stay calm. Do nothing to upset him.

I reached out, and clutched her fingers with mine. Elena watched me with curiosity. 'My family,' I whispered to her, and shrugged.

Our destination was Varenna, a small picturesque town right on the lake. After ninety minutes on the featureless motorway, it seemed fairly certain that we had overshot it by some distance. Elena had consulted a map before we left and so knew precisely where we should have turned off. She had been relaying to me the directions, which I dutifully conveyed to my grandfather, but my grandfather responded that he knew perfectly well the way, having driven it many times during his life, and long before I was born. But we were on new roads now, newly built motorway extensions. The turnings he had been anticipating no longer existed. We were driving too far north. The signs overhead pointed to Switzerland.

After two hours in this stifling car, the windows barely open a notch, the air conditioning off because the air conditioning irritated him, things were becoming testy. Empty stomachs hardly helped. At every road sign that indicated a right turn off the motorway, we spoke up, at first politely, then pleadingly. *Turn!* He drove straight past them all. We raised our voices, began shouting, his silence confounding, inexplicable. What was the matter with him? I could see a small rectangle of his face reflected in the rear-view mirror; he looked unbearably tense.

It was three o'clock now. The petrol gauge read: low.

Another exit loomed, the latest in at least a dozen we must have by now passed. It was imperative, this time, that we take it. If not, then we'd be in the tunnels that honeycombed the mountains. Beyond that, another country. I urged him into the near lane, my grandmother assisting by placing a hand on his arm as if to physically pull him into the turn. He acceded, but didn't slow down, didn't indicate. Behind us, horns, angry beeps. Abruptly, he yanked further still on the steering wheel, causing the car to cry out in distress, burning rubber. We were at last off the motorway. But now, inexplicably bypassing the nearest town, we were heading back towards Milan with what felt like murderous intent. He said nothing, my grandmother pleading that we stop somewhere, if only for a toilet break, some petrol. All the tension had settled around his shoulders. His neck must have been in knots.

Eventually, recklessly, we pulled up in a thoroughly nondescript town, half an hour from home on the banks of a river, the front wheel mounting a curb. The restaurants were closed, a single café open. It sold ice cream. We bought four. As my grandfather stalked up ahead of us, his long-suffering wife explained that the roads had confused him, frightened him. She looked gaunt and distraught herself, but desperate that we try to empathise.

'È vecchio,' she said, in apology. *He is old.*

Keen to ameliorate, Elena suggested she take a photograph of the three of us by the river. I still have the picture on my desk. It shows the three of us posing with our cones, she thin-lipped, he unreadable. None of us is smiling.

Less than fifteen minutes after we had arrived, he was ready to return home. There would be traffic soon, he warned, and he wanted to avoid it. I pointed out that there was no rush, that we were on holiday. We could hang around here for dinner, no? But soon we were back on the unfamiliar motorway, him driving in excess of the speed limit, my grandmother's hand reaching across the back of the seat again, and seeking mine.

Almost every day on Italian TV news programmes there are reports about motorway pileups, reckless driving being the national condition. By now, my grandfather seemed to be on his own collision course with his native destiny. I couldn't understand it, couldn't fathom why he would so carelessly risk our lives, couldn't comprehend what in him had broken down quite so fundamentally. His silence was thunderous, his anger expressed in the weight of his foot on the accelerator. He wanted for this to be over as soon as possible, one way or the other. He wasn't in his right mind. I was scared for him, for all of us, and begged him again to let me take the wheel. But wherever he was, he couldn't be reached. The speedometer nudged 70, 75.

We made it home, somehow, exhausted, emotional, but alive, all trace of eau de cologne long since burned off by adrenaline. I wanted to shout at him, to swear. Instead, with Elena gripping my hand as much out of relief as to quieten me, the two of us stormed off for some respite, some fresh air, a stiff drink.

∽

We returned an hour later, to find that life had already resumed its usual humdrum pattern: she bent over the low sink preparing dinner, he in the living room consumed by his crossword magazine while the television blared loudly in the background. They both looked up as we came in, both said ciao, and smiled as if nothing had happened. I was still furious enough to want confrontation, but I couldn't do it. All I saw now were these two elderly and frail people, as eminently fallible as the rest of us but perhaps more easily confused by the world around them. I knew that his disappointment at himself was greater than my anger could ever be. I held such affection for him then, for them both.

My grandmother asked me to help set the table.

Later that evening, we played cards, him teaching Elena the rules as we went along. She won the first hand with disarming ease, prompting much mute surprise from him. My grandmother was jubilant on her behalf, and offered her a boiled sweet. But then he won the second hand, so the universe, within these four safe walls at least, was righted once more, and all was well.

How to clear a table

This is achieved slowly, and carefully. Something similar might be said about every task in life, for a methodical approach reaps dividends. You are familiar with the tortoise and hare? Do not stack more than three plates at a time, and do not place plates in the sink but rather on the side of the sink, the cutlery too. Do not allow anyone else to wash up, as a job worth doing is a job worth doing well only by someone prepared to put in the necessary effort. Few do. Squirt washing up liquid onto scouring pad, and scrub each plate thoroughly, top and bottom, then rinse thoroughly – thoroughly – before placing on rack where it can drip dry, the drips caught on the rack below in an absorbent sponge layer. Squeeze the absorbent sponge layer into the sink afterwards.

Approach the tablecloth with care. Draw each corner towards the middle until it resembles something that a stork might use in which to transport newborn babies. Bunch it together, and take it to the kitchen table with all the care of a bomb disposal unit. Place the bundle onto the kitchen table, and carefully unwrap. Scrape all the bread-roll crumbs into a small pile on a side dish, then place the side dish on the window ledge for the sparrows who will be expecting their feed at no later than 1 p.m. Empty everything else in the sink, and rinse away.

Fold the tablecloth and its plastic underlay precisely, not carelessly. Carelessly means you will have to do it all again. Folds are there to be adhered to; think of them as map coordinates. Place back in drawer, then wipe down all surfaces with a damp cloth.

Check the living-room floor for further detritus, vacuum if necessary. In any event, vacuum. Better to be safe.

. . . .

three

My living family tree always was a pretty small one. There have been no uncles or aunts, no cousins, and, except for a brief time in my younger life, just the one set of grandparents. Those blood relatives that still remain are people I have little or no contact with today, and I am, I think, dysfunctionally content with that. It's all I know. It's all my children know, too, and they seem to accept their fate, although they do wish there were more presents to open at Christmas.

Any opportunity for them to enjoy the reported benefits that come from having a larger family, then, stem entirely from my wife's side, which is numerous and varied, its members spread right across north-western Spain, and down into the heavy heat of central Madrid. She sees some of them regularly, and the rest infrequently. But every last one appears to remain in perpetual touch with each other via a succession of WhatsApp groups whose activity makes her phone chime long into the night, these distant second cousins and the occasional tall niece feeling it imperative to update everybody all of the time via an array of endlessly upbeat emojis. I am far more likely today to receive an emoji-laden birthday message from one of her aunts than I am from one of those aforementioned still-living family members of my own.

It is via the use of social media that her considerable clan let one another know that distance has failed to divide them, and that no one has forgotten anyone else irrespective of wherever they may have strayed in the world. And it enhances the cliché that the family bond, at least in this case, really does retain an importance that places it hierarchically above those relationships with mere civilians.

This is important, Elena tells me. She tells me that I am missing out here, that we all need the comfort of a family – even me. She has spent much of our relationship trying to work me into hers, but her efforts have failed. Or perhaps it is *I* that have failed both her, and myself. The trouble is, I only know what I know, and my experience with family, limited as it is, has tainted my outlook on its benefits and uses. It's not that I don't like the idea of one, merely that I simply don't know what to do with my adopted one, afforded me by marriage, or where precisely I fit in. Elena's relatives, who come in all shapes and sizes, ages and temperaments, are kind and decent people, most of them, but perhaps because they have failed to learn English just as assuredly as I have not succeeded in learning their language, the barrier between us remains. A niece will arrive every so often, keen to see the capital, and at home I make an effort – the accommodating host – but it transpires that they are suffocated by shyness, and their shyness in turn suffocates me. Stalemate. In each other's company we do little more than smile awkwardly, hoping that the smile compensates for our lack of words. But it doesn't. Over the course of a few hours, it becomes increasingly strained. My cheeks begin to hurt. We remain as much strangers after their visit as we were before.

Perhaps it is defective of me to continue to take this view, to fail to make an effort that may ultimately pay off and enrich my life. I know that the problem here is me, not them. But I find it difficult to make lasting connections because I don't really know these people, and they don't know me. Our connection is ultimately a tenuous one. I feel I've reached an age in life where I am no longer prepared to feel quite so teenage in my discomfort.

This, I think, is at least one reason why I have always cherished the family members that I *have* managed to remain close to: namely, Nonna and Nonno, my grandparents.

As a child, my annual two weeks in Milan felt like nothing less than an eternity. Perhaps in a parallel universe, I am still there, still fourteen and watching Eurythmics videos on MTV, still pining for the next-door neighbour's aloof daughter, and still missing my friends at home.

As an adult, I always ensured that my trips back were short ones, long weekends at most. But even these felt like a stretch, the days yawning from morning to night in a mocking slow motion, absent of incident. And yet before every trip, even though I knew precisely what was in store (because nothing was in store), the butterflies were there. I liked that my arrival created a fuss, the air in their flat suddenly disrupted as I was clutched and kissed, my pallor judged and appraised ('Are you eating enough?'), my grandmother peppering me with questions of formality that never felt like duty: how are you, how is work, are you well? The briefest of inquisitions before equanimity was restored, and she drifted back to the kitchen, and he to the living room, leaving me in that overfamiliar limbo of: what do I do now? There were hours left in the day, after all, so how on earth was I going to fill them? Would it be rude to take out my book and start reading so soon, ruder still to leave them and go for a walk? Probably. And so I would simply sit among them, my physical presence alone seemingly enough for them both, but never quite enough for me.

I tried to acclimatise, really I did. After the torpor prompted by a typically heavy Italian lunch – the only place on earth I have ever had a siesta was in their flat after a midday meal of three courses – I would excuse myself and stretch my legs around the neighbourhood, or, if my grandfather's bike could continue to bear my weight, then a ride into Milan where for old times' sake I would cycle down Senso Unicos. But no matter how far I strayed, the need to return home by five thirty remained pressing, because dinner was at an immovable six o'clock each night, irrespective of whether or not I might be hungry then. Routine was routine, and that was that.

Each year became a little harder, each comprising of less and less incident. Fewer trips to the shops, no outings anywhere. I'd read three or four books, but itched for more activity, more stimulants. I can still see myself and my grandfather sitting in our respective chairs in the living room for hours on end, the clock ticking between us, one of us occasionally lifting our eyes to meet the other's before retreating back into our silent worlds.

I valued my time with them, always, and couldn't wait to leave.

I wonder what my impatience was hinting at. Did I want this chapter of my life to be over, for them to have given in to mortality in order to free up my social calendar? So that I wouldn't have to make these annual pilgrimages any more but rather go off, with my family, on proper holidays instead?

The answer, I'm sure, is: no. No, I didn't. But I simply didn't know how to exist in such a quiet space and at such an immobile pace, year on year. The arguments that erupted every summer in my youth had ceased after my mother had died, their absence replaced by nothing, by tumbleweed. In Milan I felt only half alive, as if left on a shelf somewhere, forgotten, desperate for my phone to work, to plug myself back in to the world and dive into its din and clatter.

I was not, I fear, a good companion for them in their later years. I wore my boredom all too evidently. I counted the hours, could barely conceal my impatience to get back home, normal service to be resumed shortly.

I used to take the 18:20 flight back from Linate to Gatwick, but increasingly I took the 14:10.

Shortly before a visit to see her great-grandmother, her own paternal grandmother having died nine years before she was born, my younger daughter, Evie, then six years old, wanted some information on what to expect. She had just started keeping a diary to alleviate her own boredom on these necessary family trips. My grandmother, now properly old, had recently been admitted into a care home against her wishes.

'How old is she?'

'Ninety-five.'

She nodded matter-of-factly, and made a note of it on the page in blue felt tip. 'So she'll be dead soon?'

'Perhaps,' I told her. 'It's possible.'

In the end, my grandfather didn't, like many Italians of all ages, die behind the wheel of a car in an accident of his own reckless making. He died from the complications that come with old age. He was ninety-four, and after a fall at home resulted in a broken leg that he chose not to inform me about because he didn't want to worry me, he was admitted into hospital. A month in, he contracted a bug which his frail body was too weak to fight.

I feared for my grandmother then. She had never been alone before, and she and her husband had spent the previous seventy years together, seven decades of love and bickering and bonding, of closely guarded secrets and a few festering open wounds they had always hoped mere sticking plasters might cover over forever and successfully conceal. They had outlived almost all their friends, and their own daughter. There was nobody left.

I missed his funeral. In Italy, they bury their dead quickly. I was in America for work, with no way of getting back in time for the service. I flew to be with my grandmother a few days later and accompanied her to the cemetery along with my grandfather's ashes, which were to be interred in a plot they had secured, I learned, many years previously. A priest was on hand to read a prayer while my grandmother watched on, her eyes pooling. I waited for her tears to spill, but they didn't. It was as if she needed to show some strength here, to prove, perhaps mostly to herself, that she could be strong without him. She remained stoic.

His passing had not taken her by surprise, for both of them had been showing conspicuous signs of slowing down for several years, each giving in to the demands made of them by their years. They left the house less and less, took fewer shopping trips to the big supermarket. He had long ago given up playing bowls when a new group of people came in – relative youngsters in their seventies – and took over, as new people do. He stopped fishing. A year previously, they had found it necessary to employ someone who came in five mornings a week to help with the daily chores. This was not a decision my grandmother took lightly, because her home and its upkeep, she believed, was her duty alone. But the kindly young Dominican woman brave enough to take over would prove patient in putting up with her exacting standards. The loss of their independence summoned up in her *many* irritations, and I began to notice them bickering more. If my grandmother had always suffered in silence, furious in so many ways at my grandfather and his peculiarities, she was silent no more. To me, she hinted at hardships in her life, employing Milanese hand movements to connote endless suffering. He would shout back, then huff and retreat into the bedroom, slamming the door behind him.

The last time I had seen them together, they didn't bother eating at the living-room table any more, deciding that it was quicker, and less fuss, simply to eat in the kitchen, both of them done with the ceremony of tradition. A significant capitulation, this, the white flag of surrender, the beginning of the end. They no longer dressed nicely, either, she spending days in her housecoat, he in a threadbare pair of sweatpants. On one occasion, I saw washing-up piled in the sink. Deferring a chore for later had been unconscionable for her, but not any more.

Into such a narrative, then, there could only ever have been one conclusion, one inevitability. But, still, a shock.

My grandfather, gone. She would now surely spiral without him.

But, no. She adapted to widowhood more easily than I might have expected. She was ninety years old by now, but still possessed of all the nervous energy she had passed down to her daughter and, in turn, to me. She was aware of her own expected trajectory, of course she was, but she was going to do her best to buck it.

How to mend socks

*S*ocks, like ancient Rome, were not built to last. The stretching of the garment, particularly around the heel area, reveals its many vulnerabilities. Holes will appear, but this does not mean it is time to purchase a new pair. Retrieve your well-stocked sewing kit and locate a thread in a similar colour to the sock – not necessarily the exact same colour because who will see a sock, except when wearing with sandals in warmer months? – then thread the needle through the cotton, ensuring to leave the knot on the inside of the sock. Slowly pull the thread to the hole's far perimeter, thereby creating a criss-cross pattern until the pattern spans its length and width. At this point, start gently to pull the thread together and close it up.

Repeat as necessary every few weeks.

four

My mother never liked them, of course. Couldn't stand them half the time, it often seemed to me. For as long as I knew them they never got on, the generational shift in her bones having swooped in early, always threatening to lift her up and away from them and their rigid, outdated morals, their life-strangling secrecies. After a childhood that left her psychologically scarred – one she very rarely spoke about to me and whose details would only be made plain long after she had died – she was plotting her escape.

My grandparents had never been particularly malleable parents. They had been horrified by my mother's love of the young Elvis, then bemused by her obsession with the Beatles. They became increasingly resistant to her learning English when they realised that this was not merely part of the school curriculum but her way to further facilitate that longed-for freedom from them, from Italy. If she became bilingual, she would be gone.

She arrived into London in the mid 1960s. I imagine that she bought a return ticket to appease and reassure them, but she never intended to go back. In England she would try hard to fully shake herself free from their influence and heavy-handed concern, to become at last her own person.

But not all dreams come true.

She didn't, at least, give into them, and she never returned. No wonder things were problematical after that. I have many memories of her coming off the phone from my grandparents on weekday evenings, after an hour and more of remonstrations, first from him, then from her, bringing my mother to tears, to shouts, to slamming down the phone. It was intriguing to witness as a ten-year-old, my mother reduced to my own status, that of a child, whose opinions couldn't possibly hope to stand alongside those of her anguished, and often furious, parents. Every phone call – and there was at least one every couple of weeks – boiled down to the same purpose: come home. Come home, because it didn't seem to them that her marriage was working; and then, later, come home, because it hadn't, he had left, it was over. They wanted to help, of course, but they went about it badly, not with empathy and sympathy but with smotherings and told-you-so's.

To have a divorced daughter was an embarrassment, the too wilfully independent daughter who had left for ever while all the other errant daughters had eventually returned, tails between legs. And now look: a divorcee whose children qualified for free school dinners because money was in such short supply, whose home was a small flat in a tower block in which people pissed in the lifts, and where break-ins were so routine that they didn't always get reported to the police.

Their daughter had made a terrible mistake. They wanted her to acknowledge this, to show penitence, to ask for their help, to *come home*.

You'd think my mother would steer well clear, perhaps permanently. And yet, every summer, it was to them that we returned like moths to the light, obligingly, out of some kind of non-negotiable necessity. The first couple of days of every visit were fine, and it was nice for our nuclear family to become an extended one once more. But soon enough routine was re-established, and true colours began to parade like peacocks as the three of them resumed their expected roles. The arguments, the recriminations, began again in earnest. 'Basta!' my mother would shout. *Enough!* This was the point at which I would take my football downstairs into the courtyard to kick it against the wall for hour after stultifying hour, waiting for the storm above to pass. Sometimes my mother would come down, too, not to join me, but for a breather, standing in the shade and fishing for a cigarette, giving me loaded looks filled with a small print I was far too young to read, much less comprehend.

She would only visibly relax on the flight back home, that same sense of freedom renewed. I would watch her as she uncoiled, re-filled her shape, as her breathing slowed. But then, without fail, something curious would happen every time we touched down at Heathrow, and made our way slowly, lugging suit-cases on tube and bus, through the centre of town, the nice bits, to our part, which was less nice. She would fall quiet, then become sad and tearful, and then, by the time we were home, inconsolable, her depression sometimes not lifting for weeks. The phone calls back home took on a different timbre during this time; they were quieter, filled with an enigmatic tenderness.

I could only grasp at how complicated life must have been for her. Was this what it was like for every-one, I wondered? So complicated, so many hurdles flung so carelessly in front of you? If this is what fam-ily did, then I wanted no part in it, if it meant being helplessly and inextricably linked to other people whose only real purpose, it sometimes seemed to me, was to make life difficult for one another.

I never knew, really, what lay at the root of my mother's strained relationship with my grandmother. I know that, as a child, she spent some time in a convent and that she hated it, that the nuns' collective evil streak was enough to convince anyone of an absence of God. Those children that wet the bed, for example, had to do laps of the nearby sports field with their thin, shamefully sodden mattresses draped on their heads while everyone else watched on. My mother frequently wet the bed.

I know that my grandparents showed their love for her in a flinty, unemotional way, critical not encouraging, closed not open, demonstrative more in anger than in kindness; products of their generation and their generation's way of doing things. They had certainly not been as affectionate to her as they subsequently were to me, but this can often be the case with grandparents. Relieved of the burden of being the primary caregiver, responsible for raising, shaping and disciplining, they can take on a much more affectionate, indulgent role with grand-kids than they ever had with their own children.

When I was in my mid teens, my mother told me that my grandfather wasn't my real grandfather, that she had been born, in 1943, in Yugoslavia ille-gitimately, her biological father unknown, at least to her. I seem to remember her telling me that my grandmother had had a relationship with an Italian soldier, and that because Italy and Yugoslavia were on opposing sides in the war, my grandmother had to flee her home in fear of being found out. She ended up in Milan where, a few years later, she met the grandfather I would never be able to think of as my *step*. He told me himself in his eighty-ninth year that he was not my biological grandfather, perhaps keen to tie up loose ends before death claimed him. I remember the moment vividly: in a mid-afternoon lull, me reading in the living room. He left his place at the table, his crossword uncompleted, and went into the kitchen where, moments later, he called for me. I went, and saw him standing alongside his wife as he made his faltering confession. He looked nervous and tentative. I realised the need to play along here, to greet this news as *news*.

'No?' I said, genuinely curious to what he might say next.

He told me what I already knew, and I waited for him – or perhaps her – to tell me a little bit about my mother's real father. But they didn't. They were already dispersing, my grandmother resuming her place at her sewing machine. The words were in my throat and, though mindful of causing offence, I asked, as best as I could in the Italian words that came to me, who my real grandfather was.

'*He* is your real grandfather,' she told me, pointing to him, a certain steel in her eyes and drawing another of her customary veils.

I understood, and promptly capitulated. I hugged my grandfather then, calling him, as if to underline the meaning behind my grandmother's point, what he had always been to me, and would always remain: Nonno.

I would still occasionally think about the man who had preceded him. But I have since read enough books on the era to know that when women became pregnant during the war, it wasn't always as the result of a rose-tinted romance.

I do not believe that my mother herself ever knew the whole story, either. It was this, I surmised, that made their relationship such a problematical one, or at least lay at its root. So many fundamental secrets – who am I? where am I from? – were never revealed to her, always denied. I imagined that my mother, as a child, might have been a painful memory for my grandmother, and was perhaps a source of shame for my grandfather who, I only found out much later, wasn't able to have children himself. I knew that he had insisted to his wife that no one ever find out he wasn't my mother's real father, and so this was the secret between them, one that swelled tauntingly over the years when friends of the family would insist that my mother, as a teen-ager, looked far more like him than she did her.

It's only now, as I have become older, that I fully come to wonder about all this. I look into my grand-mother's sweet, sympathetic face, and try to imagine all the things I don't know about her but want to know for the simple fact that they happened, because they are part of her, and their consequences are part of me. I'm fascinated about the life she lived before I lived, just as I am about my mother's, and yet here I am, at least halfway through my own life, and all I have are partial truths, half-truths and, if not outright lies, then their white counterparts, and deliberate obfuscations.

When I was nine or ten years old, I had a school-friend who lived at home with his parents and his maternal grandmother. I would often go back to his house after school to kick a football in the road until the neighbours came out to complain, at which point it was back to his for tea. I never did meet his mother and father, but 'Gran', as he called her, was a permanent fixture. I remember her as ancient, though I realise now that she was probably no older than her mid forties (the average grandparent in the UK today is just forty-eight years old; a generation ago, they would have been several years younger). She was nice and effusively generous, forever fussing around us, and making us dinners that were, to me, the very apex of decadent luxury: burgers and chips that, just half an hour previously, had been frozen solid in the Electrolux. And yet now here they were, hot and brown and steaming, on our plates. To me, someone with a health-obsessed vegetarian mother who never shopped in the freezer section of the local supermarket when she could have made something out of celery and spinach instead, this was miracle food. It tasted as it looked, and it looked *fabulous*: lumpen, hearty, proud of its calories, its unsaturated fats. 'Gran' then actually allowed us to eat it on our laps in the living room in front of the television, offering up as much ketchup as our plates could handle. She was living with them, my friend told me, because his parents were out all the time at work; essentially, she was bringing him up. This was proof to me that not all grandparents were divisive, and that not all family structures needed to be combustible. Here was a *great* grandmother, and I wanted her for myself.

Did I not remember, at that age, the age of nine or ten, that I had another set of grandparents, these ones closer to home – my paternal ones? Did I not consider that I might have a set of *great* grandparents myself? Or had I already written them off, aware that there were problems here, too, a rift on that side of the family that had long ago rendered such harmonious communal living a pipe dream, an impossibility?

Even before he left us for good, shortly before I turned eleven, my father was rarely home. He worked a lot, and his job, in the travel industry, came with a busy social life of which, it seemed, he took full advantage. So if I didn't see very much of him, I saw even less of his parents. They were from York, of Celtic ancestry, I think, and older than my maternal grandparents. In my memory, they are quintessentially British, class-obsessed, in clothes that might have contained starch. What I do know of my grandfather is that he was as unimpressed with where we had settled in London as my mother's parents had been, and the fact that we had recently moved into a newbuild council estate was confirmation that the well-educated middle-class son he had so diligently raised was now slipping inexorably down towards the working classes. This was disastrous. On those occasions we did visit him, presumably though I suppose not necessarily always with my father in tow, they proved to be awkward, stilted affairs. A stern, serious man who I can only ever picture in my mind as wearing a suit and standing upright, he discouraged me from playing with the children down the road for the reason that, in his estimation, they were ruffians. The fact that I myself was a latchkey kid from an inner-city sink estate suggested that he was perhaps delusional if he thought that I was better than they, but nevertheless he insisted I play closer to home, within eyesight of his front door and line of vision. Playing rowdily was a transgression in itself, because we didn't want to disturb the neighbours, did we? It was a nice street, orderly, the kind of place where curtains might have twitched. Their house was nice, too. They grew roses in the garden, and made marmalade in the kitchen. The uncarpeted staircase creaked, and inside the imposing wardrobe in their bedroom there lurked, of this I was sure, monsters.

I can conjure up their faces only thanks to the two photographs I still have of them tucked away in an album somewhere. In them, she is sweet and timid and thin, cheekbones and hair and self-effacement, an uncertain smile on her face and deference in her eyes; he, in stark opposition, is stiff and authoritarian, in a suit and tie and heavy-framed glasses. I want to say that the chain of a pocket watch is visible running from his double-breasted jacket, but I must be imagining this, surely? What I do remember is that he looks grave, like someone not quick to smile, his face a nineteenth-century face. Had he never existed, Dickens might have invented him. He is upstanding and upright, proper, the kind of man around whom children had to be seen and not heard. Never would he have glanced at my trousers and told me which way to dress.

Did I see them regularly while my parents were still married? Did they travel down to London much, or us up to York? Did we ever go on holiday together, to the circus, the funfair? What about the presumably nearby Yorkshire Dales? Did he ever take us urban dwellers into his own backyard countryside? I have no idea. But then neither can I bring to mind a single conversation I had with either of them. In terms of reliable memories, I do know that one year, perhaps under the conviction that all children should show musical ability, he shipped the piano from his house down to London and up to our ninth floor flat, where the journey in the dank lift doubtless insulted its delicate sensibilities. It took pride of place in our front room, a new surface on which, as long as we put coasters down first, to put coffee cups.

Here the piano sat, cruelly ignored, scant competition for the television that vied, successfully, for my attention. I never played it. I imagine I was required to write a letter of thanks, to which I presume he responded accordingly. I wish I had kept that letter. Otherwise, that's it, nothing more. They remain sadly two-dimensional in my memory, their entire lives a mystery to me, their characters and personalities mostly unrevealed. I do know that she died first, but not before, I think, Alzheimer's claimed her. There is a hazy recollection of my having visited her once in what must have been a care home, and then visiting her no more. I didn't attend either of their funerals, which I suppose means that, having never fully registered their presence, I never fully registered their absence either. My mother later told me, shortly after his funeral and her separation from his son, that my grandfather appeared to her as a ghostly vision in my bedroom one night, looking on fondly as she put me to bed. She made eye contact with him, she said, and he nodded once in a benevolent way that made her think that he was watching over us. My mother had never made such otherworldly claims to me before, and I rather wondered whether she, a teetotaller, had uncharacteristically been at the drink.

I suppose I wish they had made more of a lasting impression, but then I could say much the same about my father. That side of the family has remained mostly out of focus, and if there is blame to apportion here, there is also consequence. The maternal side of my family couldn't have failed to make a lasting impression. Distance may have been a problem, but they nevertheless worked diligently to make themselves heard: through postcards, birthday and Christmas cards, regular phone calls, annual trips, and those recurring arguments that would reliably send my mother half mad with fresh frustration. The very fact of them, these taciturn, curmudgeonly people who challenged my mother's invulnerability for as long as she lived, loomed large in my life, even if mostly on the edges. But I only had to squint to see them. I knew, early on, just as Elena says now about her own family, that they were important to me and my identity, that however much they threatened to upturn our fragile equilibrium, my link to them was something I needed to maintain, and treasure.

So I did.

When I became a father for the first time, they were the first people I called, desperate to let them know that they had made it to great-grandparenthood.

I had, months previously, Google-translated what I wanted to say in order to keep the tripping-over-tongue incidents to a strict minimum on the day itself. This proved prescient of me, because my brain was all over the place in the moments after my daughter was born. There had been blood, more than I could have possibly anticipated, and as I watched nurses alarm-call doctors, then watched as successive doctors arrived, slipping on the blood which was now arranged across the floor with all the deliberate carelessness of modern art, I realised that this was not normal, and that panic was permitted.

But once it was proved to me, beyond reasonable doubt, that the baby was okay, and breathing, and that my poor depleted wife was fine, too, our new daughter already at her breast but with little clue of what to do next, I took my cue to stride outside and into the corridor, past my mother-in-law who was already eager to bustle in and stake her claim, and dialled their number, 0039 for Italy, 02 for Milan.

It was late evening by now, and I was exhausted and emotional. Our daughter had been born on Christmas Eve, sharing the same birthday as my late mother, which made it all the more poignant for them. I can no longer remember the conversation, though I have to believe that Google served me well. There may have been tears. If my grandparents had ever been keen to become great-grandparents, this was something they never shared with me, as seemingly content to let me live my own life as they had been adamant to perpetually stage-manage my mother's. But they were happy for me, certainly. It would have been my grandmother who answered the phone, because she always did, especially in the evenings when he would already be reliably fast asleep in front of the television and not easily roused. But I'm sure that he would have been alerted, and was standing next to her as I related the news – 'a girl!' – and they probably shared the earpiece as I went on to babble whatever else came to mind. I had no idea how to convey the baby's weight, or whether I had to convert to the metric system for Italians, but they didn't ask, and so I didn't bother. But I do remember how satisfying it was to fulfil and uphold this tradition, that I was doing what people did when they became parents: they called those closest to them.

The convoluted process of actually introducing these very distant relatives to one another in person would follow later. But not too much later, given their tireless conviction that their time was almost up, and that, correspondingly, we should get a shift on and book the flights quickly.

Amaya was just three months old when we went. I registered more than my usual palpable growing excitement as we made the familiar approach through their quiet neighbourhood in this newly unfamiliar manner: pushing a pushchair. They buzzed us in through the main gate, then rushed to the kitchen window to see us arrive, waving from their third floor flat as we walked through the car park and towards the block. I had thought that perhaps they might scale the stairs to meet us outside, but, no, they stayed where they were, at their front door, my grandmother now peering over the banisters as she watched Elena and I awkwardly rearrange the bags on our back and secure the nappy-changing bag, then as I scooped up our sleeping daughter from the pushchair, careful not to wake her (I didn't want their first view of her to be of her crying), which allowed Elena to fold it and jam it awkwardly under one arm, before we began to negotiate the steps carefully together, one by one by one.

It was to prove a curiously anticlimactic visit, but then I'm not quite sure what I was expecting. Had I been anticipating fuss, frenzied levels of interest, excitement, my grandparents nothing less than revitalised by the new life I had helped create? It didn't happen. They smiled a lot, certainly, but the moment our daughter roused from slumber, they both took a step back and left us to it. She was nervous when my grandfather held his great-granddaughter in his arms, which made him nervous too, and rigid, and even more keen to give her back as quickly as possible. At times, they looked like strangers in their own home, and it became clear to me then that this was perhaps simply too much new life to introduce into such small and silent quarters, their home's carefully freighted balance disrupted in ways that neither of them could fully cope with any more, nor wanted to. Strength was required here, a strength that had perhaps dissipated years before.

They would both go on to take great interest in our daughters, but at arm's length, and they would always prominently display the photographs we would send to them, dutifully passing them around to neighbours and friends. In this way they managed to appreciate the continuation of their lifeline, albeit in the only way they knew how: from a distance.

I felt obscurely disappointed. But then perhaps this is what it's like when you are really old, when you are *great,* and not merely *grand*parents.

Grandparents themselves, of course, are a different ball game altogether. Grandparents have dibs on the new arrival, as I was to find, and are not afraid to prove it.

How to air a bed

Bacteria festers in hot and hidden folds and crevices, so beds need airing daily. Your mother learned this; you should too. Pass this information on to Elena. Upon rising, fetch the clothes dryer from the side of the wardrobe and place it at the end of the bed. Pull the cover sheet straight across the length of the bed and drape it onto the clothes dryer, then repeat with the blanket and the sheet underneath. Make sure the blanket and sheets are straight and neatly laid out, and completely off the mattress. Open the balcony doors to allow the room to air, but close the bedroom door to prevent it slamming. Leave the air to circulate for no less than one hour irrespective of the season. Then return and make the bed, and make it properly: tight, and neat, and crease-free.

five

When Elena's mother became pregnant with her, it wouldn't have dawned on her to seek advice from outsiders, or a book, and Mumsnet in the 1970s was a kernel in nobody's imagination. When she did give birth for the first time, she relied almost exclusively on her own mother for everything, and her mother duly obliged.

By the time Elena was the same age as her mother had been when she gave birth to her, she had already graduated from university with a degree in science, and was preparing to come to London for six months in order to learn English and widen her horizons. It was here, during her second week of serving coffee in a Soho dive where the management had wandering hands and the late-night clientele came on to her by boasting about penis size, that we met. Because she was due to return to both Spain and her boyfriend by the summer, our time together was only ever going to be short, an illicit fling. It was a good fling, though; both of us enjoyed it. A dozen years later, with us on to our second mortgage and Elena now pregnant, we had to finally admit to one another that perhaps it was going to be more lasting than that.

If we were now to become parents, it also signified something that seemed to unfold rapidly across a much broader canvas: her mother was about to become a grandmother. In the run-up to this event, she was an exclamation mark in human form, her eyebrows perpetually halfway up her forehead in anticipation of the happy event.

I am going to do my level best here to steer clear of the kind of material that was routinely doled out by stunted stand-up comedians of the 1970s, so I will simply say that her mother had always been accepting of her daughter's independence, but I do think she was daunted by her intelligence. She was not to be feared so much as sympathised with. And it seemed she had never been entirely happy that Elena failed to return to Spain, nor that she had chosen to settle in a foreign country with a man either reluctant or incapable, very likely both, of learning her language.

By the time we were expecting our first daughter, my mother-in-law had been a widow for two years, and was enjoying a second wind in life that she surely deserved. She was partly retired and so announced to us that she would come to help for the birth, and could remain with us for as long as was required afterwards. This was not fulfilling any particular request from us so much as it was her simply following her own destiny, her own maternal right. Spanish families, after all, are traditionally tightknit affairs, and domineering mothers can make for suffocating grandmothers. By comparison, of course, I had come from a splintered nuclear family, and clung on to my independence protectively. To suggest that I was not much looking forward to her arrival is an understatement.

Our relationship was already well established as a fairly spectacularly dysfunctional one. With no common tongue between us, we had spent the previous dozen years barely communicating at all. The moment it became clear to her that I was never going to be fluent in Spanish was the moment she gave up on me. On visits to Spain, I was easily and conveniently overlooked, mere baggage that came along with her daughter on annual visits, and when she came to London, I was the slightly sinister landlord under whose roof she was required to live. She was not to blame for our situation; we both were. Although I always knew her heart was in the right place, she seemed to me to be overly blunt, frequently rubbing me up the wrong way, and overly sensitive too, taking offense when I had intended none. In her company, I became diffident and awkward, the stilted shyness she prompted within me coming across, to her, as steely aloofness. I was not at my best around her, and although I hated coming across in this way I could find no way to change it. Eye contact unnerved me, so I avoided it. Thrown together, we were territorial cats stalking our prey, Elena, my wife, but *her* daughter. The impulse to hiss in one another's direction was felt keenly by us both.

I realise, of course, that the poor woman was simply pining for her daughter, heartbroken that the family unit had been so carelessly, and summarily, disbanded. The fact that we were about to have a child must have amplified her sense of distress. I have enough self-awareness to realise that were the situation reversed, I'd have felt much as she did. When my daughters grow up, leave me and find partners who tempt them to another part of the world, I will make it my life's work to make their partners' lives hell, because they will have broken my heart, too.

The tensions between generations never seem to go away, wherever you come from. When I speak to a friend, Sumathi Senthil, a second-generation Indian who now lives on the outskirts of London, she paints for me a family portrait that is at once similar to mine in that it is both complex and complicated, but also quite distinct. Her story makes me reassess my own, and realise that whatever complaints I might have, it could be worse.

'In India,' she says, 'it is traditional to live in joint families. So the daughter-in-law would have moved into the parents' house, and the parents would have remained the head of the family. This would have given them all sorts of privileges, among them the right to name their children's children.' Sumathi laughs. 'Something that, over here in England, people would never be able to tolerate.'

But even Indian family culture is being gradually unpicked by insidious Western influence. 'It's true to say that in-laws don't live with their children so much any more, but even then, grandparents – and particularly grandmothers – still do remain a crucial part of daily life.' She explains that her husband remains close to his mother, despite arguments so frequent they are practically mandatory, this being the only way they find they can communicate. The whole family, she says, is required to see her once a week, while she, Sumathi, the dutiful daughter-in-law, speaks to her every day, and routinely does her shopping for her, irrespective of the fact that the woman is still fit and healthy enough to do her own groceries. In Sumathi's depiction of her, she sounds like a creation right out of Roald Dahl, someone whose satisfaction only comes, cruelly, at the cost of everybody else's frustration.

We compare notes, and I tell her about my mother-in-law. Nodding, she says: 'I suppose that certain societies and their cultures put you in a position where such situations are unavoidable, and in Asian circles there is this expectation that you will tolerate anything, any behaviour, if it comes from somebody who is within the family – aunties, uncles, brothers-in-law, grandparents – no matter how annoying they might be. Over here, in the West, we are more likely to say, "Sod this, I'm not having it, I'm off down the pub." In India, you simply put up with it.'

I suggest to her that she must be envious of Western attitudes, when things could be so much easier for her. She thinks about this for a while, then says: 'Sometimes I am envious, yes, because I suppose that life would be easier, or at least quieter. But then, despite everything I've said about Asian families, I do believe that they are richer, in the end. They are richer because of the relationships you have within them, good and bad. Are they perfect? No. They are flawed in lots and lots of ways.' She shrugs. 'But it's family, and if you can't rely on your family in life, then who can you rely on?'

She has a point, because if I found a changing dynamic among friends after having had children – losing a support network I had naïvely believed I might have for life – then who exactly would take their place?

My wife, smiling with wisdom, had the answer.

'Your mother-in-law, of course. Get used to it.'

She arrived from Spain a week before the due date, in a winter's coat and much fervent expectation. Her suitcase was enormous. It required two hands to lift it.

We had just moved house, and had landed in an unfamiliar part of town that made the unfamiliarity we already felt at being prospective parents all the more bewildering. But while we flailed, she was all focus and drive, and addressed herself to the matter at hand with the brisk efficiency of someone who had been biding her time for this very event all along. She attended to her daughter, and readied the house for its new arrival by dusting, polishing, ensuring that the new pushchair was fully functional, that we had a sufficient stock of nappies, the right nappies, the right wet wipes, that our towels were soft enough and the IKEA cot suitably sturdy.

Each evening would close in the same fashion, her talking to her daughter at great length in largely one-sided conversations at the kitchen table, filling her in on family updates and what sundry neighbours were up to back at home. I would be in the living room in front of the TV. They were long evenings.

The due date came and went, and if Elena was made impatient by this, heavy and fatigued and ready for it all to be over, then it was nothing on how her mother felt, nervous kinetic energy forever bouncing off her, her frustration wrapped around a helpless anxiety and a craving for things to *begin*. When, four days later, we finally found reason to go to the hospital, Elena had to tell her, between early contractions, that unlike in Spain she would not be welcome in the delivery room itself, and that she would have to content herself with pacing the corridor outside. This did not go down well, and it was all she could do not to challenge NHS bureaucracy in her harshest Castilian.

Amaya's arrival was as monumental as any new child's, and no more; this curious small creature, almost definitely human yet somehow thoroughly alien. *Ours.* Though she swiftly prompted within us the everyday miracle of parental love, it would take time to get used to her presence in our lives. We hadn't done this before; it felt, in the most fundamental of ways, new. Not for my mother-in-law. For her, the connection was immediate and instantaneous, a splash of the very brightest colour in her otherwise monochrome life. If possession is nine-tenths of the law, then she possessed our daughter entirely while we, her granddaughter's parents, waited our turn, first patiently, then, after a while, not so much. We became a bad sitcom routine, impervious to the canned laughter.

For the first few weeks of our daughter's life, my mother-in-law exerted a level of attention towards her that would have impressed the Stasi. She was behaving in an elemental fashion that she appeared incapable of harnessing, of reining in; her own daughter could only watch on in a bewildered fashion.

She was eerily attuned to the slightest sigh from our baby girl, and fussed over her with what seemed to me, to us both, to be endlessly dramatic overtures. She watched over her while she slept in her cot, and while Elena breastfed. On those occasions when my daughter was in my arms, I was aware of her constant appraisals as to how I was holding her, supporting her, rocking her. When friends came over to do what all good friends must when one of their number has a baby – coo and cuddle before beating a hasty retreat – she would politely withdraw to another room until she could bear the separation no longer, at which point she would hasten into the kitchen, powered by a forward momentum of urgent limbs, swoop down on the baby being held by the friend and whisk her away. The initial moments after this happened for the first time was yet more bad sitcom slapstick, each of us looking to one another in turn, and then down to the baby-shaped absence, as if her disappearance were an illusion, a trick. And then we laughed, because, really, what else were we supposed to do?

On the occasion of our first outing together, a gentle stroll to the shops in freezing January, our daughter so bound up against the cold that only her nose was visible beneath padded cotton and flammable polyester, my mother-in-law and I managed to squabble over who got to push the pushchair.

Fallout was inevitable. Elena and I began to fight over her continued presence in our house, our lives, both of us wanting our space back, but only one of us – *her* – charged with the unenviable task of having to tell the woman to just back off a little, to let us breathe.

There were more tears that night.

My mother-in-law was with us for six weeks. Seven times six is forty-two, which means she was in our house and lives for forty-two days and forty-two nights. I could take this further, and suggest that forty-two times two is eighty-four, but I've made my point, I think: a *long* time. For each of us, for all sorts of reasons, it proved to be the longest six weeks we had endured, and while that time no doubt served to knit us all together in what ostensibly remained a common goal, it also ensured that she and I would always remain at odds, I forever the obstacle in her path in what would otherwise be unimpeded grandparent access, and transcendent happiness.

When the time came, finally, for her to go back to Spain, I was as relieved to see her go as I believe she was relieved to be going. I thanked her, sincerely, for all her help, and she responded with a level of emotion I hadn't anticipated, telling me that she would always be here to help whenever we needed her; all we had to do was ask. In that moment, I felt ashamed for the passively aggressive way in which I had behaved towards her, and I resolved to make more of an effort in the future, realising, too, how important her role would be in the life of my daughter and, later, my second daughter, and that given the absence of my own mother, she would be the only grandmother they'd have. It was a relationship we would all do well to nurture.

My daughters are now twelve and ten. Curiously, they are going through much the same experience as I did with my own grandparents: separated by hundreds of miles, and complicated by language barriers. They see each other infrequently, and when they do it takes time for them to pick up from where they had left off. This does not appear to trouble my daughters, but I'm sure my mother-in-law must feel the separation keenly. She wants to see more of them, to play a bigger role in their lives.

Perhaps she's worried that if she doesn't manage to bond with them while they are still young, she might never do so fully. She is now a grandmother six times over, her sons having become fathers in the last few years, but the role remains a complicated one, more so, it seems, than motherhood was for her. Times have moved on, and apron strings have loosened. She phones Elena regularly to express her upset about not seeing enough of her grandchildren, and Elena soothes where she can, and just listens patiently when words will not suffice. Her fate is the most dreadful one: she has had children who have had the temerity to become free of her.

We have failed her, clearly. Asian families would not look kindly upon us. These days she rarely comes to visit. When she did still come over, during school holidays, she wanted to take exclusive charge of the children in order, she implied, to give us a break, but the girls seemed reluctant to be left alone with her. They complained that they didn't like her cooking, or the fact that she served lunch at three and dinner at nine, instead of twelve and six as they were used to. Both were self-conscious about speaking Spanish with her, and they found her constant ministrations awkward and embarrassing.

Elena makes biannual trips back to Spain now to ensure that the connection is kept active. But even there, my children don't fawn over her as much as she would like, perhaps because, in Spain, they are spoiled with relatives, a great many of them closer in both age and temperament. That connection, then, is faltering. Will it, in time, improve? Will my daughters grow to be more sympathetic towards her, more understanding and kinder to this woman whose needs sit so clearly on her face, in her eyes, this ultimately well-intentioned grandmother who just wants to be loved by her grandchildren in the way she so clearly loves them?

How to honour and respect

Y*ou should be mindful, please, to extend certain common courtesies towards us. You may have* grown up and moved on, as is the nature of these things, but <u>we</u> have remained. We are still here. Think about that. We are still here in the place that you left us – home – and you can be assured that we are mourning your absence.

It's not that we want to intervene at every possible juncture of your life, because we don't. Enough to be included. We want to hear when things are going well, and when things are going badly. (We might be able to help if things are going badly.) We want more than post-cards from golden beaches in July, and Christmas cards in December. We want to hear your voice regularly, to *be reminded that we are remembered, and that you still care, that we still matter, and have a place in your adult lives. We can come for Sunday lunch; we can fly over whenever convenient; we can talk on the phone. Ideally, we'd like to be consulted, conferred with, included; we know a lot about childcare, remember? We are here for you, always here.*

Most importantly, please don't let us drift too far apart. Don't fall silent.

And if we text you, text back. A text message is never rhetorical.

. . . .

six

My mother's death at fifty-six robbed me of the opportunity of seeing what kind of grandmother she would have made, but I feel that she would have been every bit as doting, and demanding, as Elena's. She was long gone when my daughters were born, but that didn't stop me casting around and looking for her, wishing that she were here, that she would come back, to impose herself upon our lives, and for grandmotherhood to give her life a renewed sense of purpose. My girls,

I know, would have been much entertained by her, and loved her.

In her absence, I naïvely thought that my grand-parents would simply step in. I don't know what the Italian for 'great-grandparents' is, so I believed that they would simply be to my children what they had always been to me.

What I didn't account for, blindly, was that life really was changing as emphatically for them as it was for me. They were becoming slower in their movements, they ached more, and confided in me more about it. They slept poorly, shuffling around the flat at night like ghosts, and lost their appetite; mealtimes had lost all sense of occasion. I remem-ber seeing my grandmother without her teeth early one morning, and I reeled in shock, having had no idea that this eighty-something woman now wore dentures. It was confirmation to the part of me that refused to see them for what they really were: old and human after all, and that deterioration had set in. My horror at the discovery of dentures matched her own. She yelped, dashed into the bathroom to pop them back in and no more was said about it, another veil to draw over the heavy reality that hung between us.

My grandfather's own slow decline had been easier to spot. He ventured out hardly at all, and spent more and more of each day in the living room, his sole activity the crosswords he continued to attempt in front of the television. But now he fell asleep far more frequently before completing them, pen still in hand, glasses askew, mouth wide open until his wife, drawn by the snores, came in and closed it. He started conspicuously to avoid the grocery shopping, insisting that he would make do with whatever was still in the cupboards and fridge, and that, besides, he had little appetite any more.

At his wife's encouragement, he did leave the flat with semi-regularity, downstairs to the block's basement, where each flat had a small cantina, an unadorned concrete room in which tenants stored bicycles, wine, bottled water, general detritus and workbenches. Here he would potter among his tools, listening to a radio that was stymied by poor reception, until his wristwatch, as old as me, told him that dinner was looming.

We continued, diligently and dutifully, to visit, first with one daughter, then with both, but each time failed to attain any kind of success or satisfaction for either party. We were the circus that came to town, invited and yet perhaps just a little unwelcome because of all the chaos, the noise, the too many bags, the sporadic night-time cries, the unpleasant smells. They would be forced to give up their bedroom and sleep on the pull-out bed and the sofa in the living room, and their room would become, for her, unrecognisable in its mess of baby-necessary paraphernalia, the floor littered with our many clothes. They also had to contend with the occasional bared breast at feeding time, and were reliably disturbed at night when one of the children got a temperature of 101, causing panic in us all at the belated realisation that the Calpol had not been packed. Mealtimes were calamitous in a manner that is only ever funny in hindsight, every dropped plate and spilled juice registering in my grandmother's eye as a flash of pain, a wrong that had to be righted and, surprisingly, a grudge to be nurtured. I did not see the grudges coming.

I'm fairly sure that my grandfather had never changed a nappy in his life, nor had he pushed a pram. Fair enough: he was a man of his time, as most men were. He would tell me, not so much boastfully as matter-of-factly, that he had never cooked for himself, not even an egg, and though he could fix the stove when it broke down, actually frying anything on it was something that would never have occurred to him, for the simple reason that he didn't need to. There were people to do that for him, specifically women, more specifically still, his wife.

I told him, hoping to find humour in our generational differences, that at home Elena was the one far more likely to fix the cooker while I boiled myself an egg, but he didn't laugh. His eyes simply found mine over the frame of his reading glasses and appraised me for a swollen moment before, with tortoise-like gravity, he blinked and looked away.

Throughout his long life, he remained deliberately disengaged from the whole messy business of family, at one remove from its coalface. When I went to visit them once, taking with me my three-year-old daughter while Elena stayed at home with the baby, he reacted with unambiguous bemusement, eyebrows arranged in quizzical arches, intrigued as to how I thought I could possibly manage a small child in the absence of its mother. Later, he announced his mild shock when he learned that it was me who picked my daughters up from school each afternoon, tended to them, and cooked them dinner before their mother came home from the office late in the evening. As he shook his head, I wondered who he might be shaking it for: for the feminine burdens I had to shoulder, or for all that he himself had missed out on?

Previously, when parents aged and became grandparents, their new roles essentially mirrored their old ones, the woman expected to reprise her maternal instincts towards her grandchild while the man would dutifully live up to his gender stereotype by finding something interesting to occupy his waking hours, quite possibly in the garden shed. But today's generic Grandad is no longer impervious to the increasing merging of roles. In much the same way that the New Man epithet turned out, mostly, to have actual substance within the parental structure – in other words, wasn't merely a neat but empty media-coined term invented to help sell push-chairs with go-faster stripes and fat tyres – so New Grandfathers are increasingly beginning to assert themselves as secondary caregivers alongside their female counterparts. A recent survey suggested that 42 per cent of British grandfathers now regularly care for their grandchildren, compared to 45 per cent of grandmothers.

I couldn't find any statistics for great-grandparents.

During one of our last visits, no less memorable or tortured than the rest, my grandmother beckoned me into the kitchen to show me a small mark on one of the kitchen cabinets, a smudge of indelible black barely discernible to the naked eye just below the handle. Subtleties between us have often been strained, a consequence of our great age gap and cultural differences, so I couldn't for the life of me understand why she was pointing out this ancient cupboard to me, or what possible significance it might represent.

'Amaya,' she said, offering up an entirely disingenuous smile.

She explained that the last time we were there, my daughter, then three, had inflicted this permanent damage. She had noticed it immediately, and clearly didn't forget it. In relaying this news to me, a year on, she seemed to gain satisfaction of a kind, and to prove to me that she still missed nothing and noticed everything. She needed me to realise this. When she had finished talking, but continued to point to the offending mark, a curious sensation bubbled up in my ribcage: resentment, anger at her inflexibility, her sheer pettiness. I saw then what my mother had always seen in her: a minor tyrant set in her ways; a holder of tiny grudges, each of which would ultimately require airing. There was a sense here of point-scoring satisfaction, and I didn't like it.

In that moment, the dynamic shifted. I was their grand*child* no longer.

The next time we visited, we stayed in a hotel. I had expected upset, even uproar: why on earth shell out for a hotel when we could stay with them for free? But it didn't come. They obviously thought it a good idea. The equilibrium that had survived between us, and sustained us, for four long decades had gone. My new family was too combustible for them. We were a disruption. Things would never be the same again.

And things weren't. He died, and she began to deplete, a victim at last of the old age that she had for so long outrun but which had now caught up with her.

She was determined not to buckle. Widowhood at her age was more inevitability than tragedy. Shirking the black garb of mourning, she would simply adapt, and plough on, alone.

In the week following her husband's death, she attempted to prove this to me, on a day that would start with optimism but would end under a dark cloud.

'Let's go out,' she announced shortly after break-fast, which we ate together, in the kitchen.

Let's go out. These were words she had never really said to me before. We would make trips to the local supermarket, of course, and many years earlier we might have gone to see friends of theirs for an occasional Sunday lunch, much to my grandfather's instinctive displeasure. But never would we simply have gone 'out' for the sake of it. I couldn't imagine what she had in mind.

Transforming herself as every Italian woman must before they step over the threshold of their front door and into the public arena, she emerged from her bedroom looking impossibly elegant in a blouse, a pair of cotton trousers, a chiffon scarf, pearls around her neck and a reliable whiff of perfume, then grabbed me by the hand, stopping only to consult the sky from the kitchen window. An endless expanse of dazzling blue was framed within it. She frowned.

'We'll take the umbrella, just in case,' she told me.

And then we were off. *Out.*

We were going to see an old friend of hers, also a recent widow who lived in the very centre of the city. My grandfather may have been dead, but his car remained out of bounds, and so we took public transport, a first for the two of us together. The walk to the Metro station took twenty minutes, and she powered ahead as if late for the office, forcing me to lengthen my own stride in order to match her shorter but quicker one. I suggested we stop for a coffee en route, and she surprised me by saying yes. It was an obscurely lovely sensation to be doing something so ordinary with her, at the counter in a bustling café alongside suited businessmen and women, the majority of them smoking cigarettes and speaking loudly enough to suggest that the average Italian was hard of hearing.

I tried to engage her in a conversation, but she was distracted, almost agitated. Whatever it was she was processing in her head, she was doing so privately. Her coffee was devoured in two gulps, and already she was heading back out on to the street, expecting me to follow. The umbrella, perhaps inevitably, had been reliably forgotten, left on the counter. By the time she realised, we were several blocks away. She sent me back for it, with an instruction.

'Run.'

The widow's flat was tiny, and even more sparsely furnished than my grandparents'. Its mantelpiece was filled with photographs of the husband she had recently lost – a gaunt looking man with a pronounced number eleven between his eyebrows – and the grandchildren she rarely saw. She greeted me like a long lost son, and I remembered her from my childhood, an ebullient, vivacious woman who liked to squeeze the cheeks of young children and feed them *crostata*. She had aged a hundred years since I had seen her last, and was now dressed in the formulaic black of Italian widows everywhere, like someone out of a Fellini film. A bitter melancholy infused her, with good reason. She was angry with her children, furious for having been left alone. 'They barely visit,' she told me. The coffee she poured for us at her uneven kitchen table tasted of despair.

I sat in silence as I watched them leaf through old photograph albums. The widow sighed frequently. 'La vita,' she said, referring, I supposed, to her present situation, unavoidable in life, something that comes to us all eventually if we are unlucky to live long enough.

But then, suddenly, she brightened. She went to one of her cupboards and retrieved several envelopes, each containing more family photographs, black-and-white and sepia-toned, yellowed with age. Finding what she was looking for, she brought it to me now and presented it onto the kitchen table with a flourish.

It took me a while to realise what I was looking at: my mother and father on their wedding day, about to step into a waiting car. This must have been the mid 1960s, my mother looking like Mary Quant, my father in his skinny tie, both of them smiling, frozen in the moment, unaware of what lay in store for the both of them, separately. I was surprised to find a catch in my throat; I had never seen this photograph before, perhaps because, after they split up, my mother got rid of all the photographs of my father. In this one, she was radiant and beautiful.

I had no idea why the widow had such a picture, but decided that it was a gift, from her to me.

'I can have this?' I asked hopefully.

'Scusi, no,' she replied, picking it up and putting it back into its envelope, and back into the cupboard.

On the way back home, I suggested to my grandmother that we be tourists. It had been years since she had visited the city centre, even longer since she had seen Il Duomo, the astonishing cathedral and the one thing that any tourist in Milan makes a beeline towards. I thought we might go and take a look now, and after that could stroll up to the Castello Sforzesco. I could get her an ice cream there, by the fountains.

But she appeared to be in a hurry to get home, and no longer wanted to walk. One of the city's rackety old trams, its orange paint faded with age, was approaching. I explained that we could take this to the Metro station, and continue our journey from there. Milanese trams are beautiful relics in the way that so much of its architecture is. And so while you wonder how some of the buildings remain upright, similarly you can hardly believe that these modes of transport still function. But, squealing on their tracks like animals in torture as they round the bends, they do.

Relics, however, are not designed for people with mobility issues, and the step up onto the high platform proved too high for my grandmother. I had to steady her from behind, and a passenger had to pull her up from the front so that she could board. This passenger helped with the kind of perfunctory good grace that didn't seem to expect a thank you, which was a relief, because he didn't get one, not from her. Once safely aboard, she went straight to the nearest seat, and turned to face the window.

'Tutto okay?' I asked her.

She turned to look at me. Perhaps she was trying to convey something to me in her implacable gaze, but it didn't penetrate.

It was similarly novel being on a train with her, a journey I had taken countless times over the years back to their neighbourhood, but never with her. She sat primly, Miss Jean Brodie with her knees drawn together. Silently she appraised the compartment's passengers, the gaggle of girls crowded around their phones and giggling, the boys in their low-slung jeans and high-waisted boxer shorts, tattoos crawling up their bare arms and onto the

domes of their shoulders. A Roma beggar working her way up and down the carriage, dirty palm
upraised in supplication.

When we got off, I offered her my elbow, into
which she slipped her left hand, and as she gripped,
I noticed the pale gold of her wedding band, a relic
in itself. We walked together towards the exit until
we were faced with a flight of stairs and an ascend-
ing escalator. I steered her towards the latter.

What happened next happened in the most
wretched slow motion. I cannot believe that my
grandmother had never come across an escalator
before, but she didn't seem to know how to use it,
standing at first in the middle before I encouraged
her over to one side, and suggested she hold on
to the handrail. As it ascended, she fell backwards
and onto me. Her feet had been poorly positioned,
and so as the staircase rose, she toppled. I might
have expected her body to go rigid, or for her to

let out a cry of panic. But she didn't. She remained completely inert, giving in silently and resignedly to gravity. I caught her in my arms, but the curve of her spine made purchase difficult, and so the falling continued, inch by inch by inch. She was heavy, heavier than I could have anticipated, and I almost fell back myself. I crouched down, and in this way found myself cradling her head in my hands. I looked down into her inverted face, and she looked back up at mine still without any discernible expression whatsoever. Later, I would ponder over just how unusual her reaction was, how supplicant she remained. But only later.

Looking up now, I shouted out for help, relieved that I remembered the word in Italian for help. 'Aiuto!' Adding, in English, and out of desperation, 'For Christ's sake, help!'

Someone hit the emergency stop. The sound of metal on metal. A woman behind me rushed towards us, attempting to help lift the deadweight of her, while from ahead a man came rushing back down. Together, the three of us righted her, and helped her carefully up the remaining steps. People asked if she was alright, whether she was hurt. An underground employee came striding purposefully over. But my grandmother was already off, beetling towards the exit, then the underpass, then the stairs up to the street and out into open sunshine. I apologised to everyone, and thanked them, and rushed to catch up with her.

We walked home in a deliberate silence. Something had happened here, comparable to my grandfather's motorway madness, and perhaps similarly significant. Today would have implications for her future independence, her ability to be out in the world

131

after I had gone back to mine. It had been an experiment, and it had failed. This was widowhood, then: not the anticipated opening of doors, a chance to reclaim the life that had perhaps been denied to her by her late and controlling husband, but rather a slamming shut of the door behind him. My grandfather had been right: out there was too confusing for them now, and she had been foolish to ever think otherwise.

At home, she assumed her position at the kitchen sink. We ate our dinner and made no mention of the day's adventures. She looked smaller to me then, cowed. She looked what she was: ninety years old, and all alone. Was she seeing what I was seeing: that this was how it was to be from here on in? Less able, more reliant, not on me but on others, neighbours, home helps, strangers, nurses. She would be alone now. Things would get progressively worse, and then things would end.

We began to play cards, out of habit, a game more suited to three players than two. Neither of us really got into it. Distractedly, she told me she was tired, and shuffled off to the bedroom, leaving me to clear up the cards and put them away. She had never done that before.

One afternoon, shortly after the home help had left for the day, she tripped and fell to the floor of the living room, later telling me that she quite clearly heard a bone in her leg snap. She lay there with the most dreadful patience, unable to reach the phone or call for help, until well after dinner time when the elderly neighbour's own home help, a strapping Polish woman, looked in on her as she did every evening. She promptly called an ambulance.

Much as had happened with my grandfather, I didn't find out about this for several weeks. 'I didn't want to worry you,' was what she told me on the phone, a typical refrain so frequently employed by her it made me wonder once again how much else in their lives had taken place without my knowledge. They never wanted to bother me, only to exchange pleasantries in the hope of confirming that all was well, always forever, boringly, well. This frustrated me enormously, but I suppose I must have acted in kind, because to even confess to them I had something as trifling as a cold was to ignite within them panic and anxiety – how would I cope, with work, with family life? – so whatever difficulties I was going through was never conveyed to them, either.

Once I learned of her hospitalisation – she had fallen because she'd had a stroke – I booked the earliest flight out, and spent the next few days beside her hospital bed, then returning at night to her flat, alone. It is a curious sensation to be in your grandparents' home when they are no longer in it. I kept expecting ghosts, or at least the sensation of ghosts, but all I felt, keenly, was their absence. I boiled my spaghetti on her cooker in nine minutes flat, ate and washed up my dish in five, and wished she were here.

It was anticipated, if never fully articulated, that like her husband before her, she would not be coming out of hospital, that she was by now deep into the injury time of life, and that this particular injury would close curtains on her. But this Slavic woman had confounded expectation before, and would again. From the hospital she was transferred to a rehabilitation centre, where over the next several weeks she began slowly to walk again, her leg healing when, strictly speaking, it wasn't supposed to, and then she was sent home. For a time, all was well. At least I believed all was well. There may have been more strokes, more lonely incidents that accompany advanced age, but I never got to hear about them. What I did hear, from a close family friend, the *sole* surviving family friend, was that her memory was getting progressively worse. She would go shopping in the morning by herself sometimes, despite the home help's offer, and forget how to find her way back to the flat. The grocer, the baker, had to come out from behind their counters and steer her in the right direction.

It became increasingly clear that she needed a live-in nurse, and round-the-clock assistance. Her finances, however, wouldn't cover that, and neither could mine. An alternative was required. I liaised with the family friend, trusted and much loved, who told me that my grandmother would partly qualify for care-home assistance, and that her small pension would cover the rest of it. It seemed an awful, if viable, necessity, and after long discussions between the three of us, the inevitable was agreed upon: my grandmother would give up her flat of the past half century and transfer into a nearby nursing home.

There was a waiting list here, but waiting lists at care homes move faster than waiting lists do elsewhere. After a week which saw a number of hearses pull up outside their gates, a space had become available. It was at this point that she had an abrupt change of mind. She did not, now, want to move into a care home at all, of this she was adamant. She wanted to stay at home, come what may. This was all she knew: she wasn't moving.

And who could blame her? In her position, would I want to go into a care home? Would anyone?

When you are young, or at least younger, you often wonder how you yourself might feel when you get, as Diana Athill put it, somewhere towards the end. What value will you place on your remaining months and years, and how do you then define quality of life for the time that is left? When you become pronouncedly old, as my grandmother, at ninety-three, then was, would you still want to extend your days into months, even years, in order to squeeze all the remaining juice from them? Or, in the face of a future sitting in a shared institution in which you are no longer autonomous, would you instead opt for the alternative: remaining independent at home and, due to your advanced infirmity, in likely peril?

I could have told her what I felt in my heart, that she should indeed stay on in her own flat if she wanted to, and continue to make do with part-time help, and that if she fell again, as she surely would, and that if that fall ended up precipitating a possibly *final* visit to the hospital, then at least she had remained within a familiar environment, her home, for as long as she could.

But I had never had those sorts of conversations with her, and I was not about to start now. Instinctively, I felt that this wasn't my place; someone in their forties can have no idea of what it feels like to be in your eighties, your nineties. I couldn't imagine what she was going through: her resolve, her fear, her dread. Advice from me in this regard would have been glib, and in my grandmother's darkest hour I didn't want to be glib. She needed her daughter, not her grandson.

The family friend made a case on my behalf, weighing up the daily hazards of being alone for so many hours versus the comparative security of knowing that your growing needs were taken care of. She tried to explain, carefully, that when one was 'lucky' enough to reach such a grand old age, then independence simply had to come to its conclusion.

Though my grandmother quickly came to regret her decision – and, in casting around for someone else to blame, chose to blame the long-time family friend whom she never spoke to again – she moved into the care home a few days before Christmas 2013.

We went to see her shortly afterwards, leaving the girls with my mother-in-law. There, in Italy, I encountered someone I hadn't met before, a virtual stranger. My distress at this matched her own.

The home was a ten-minute drive from her flat, a distant perimeter of the neighbourhood near the train station. It was quiet here, the distance to the main road longer. There were trees. For a comparatively unattractive area, it was almost if not quite bucolic.

My first sensation was one of relief, any fears that it was as awful as she had indicated on the phone quickly assuaged. The place looked functional and clean, and there was a smell faintly redolent of school halls moments after lunch hour, and hospitals at any hour. When I approached reception and smiled at a member of staff, she looked up from her keyboard and smiled back.

It was one o'clock in the afternoon, and everybody, I was told, would be upstairs in the main hall. We took the lift. The main hall was large and airy, full of windows looking out onto gardens, and what may have been birch trees. Against the walls were arranged perhaps as many as forty chairs, upon each of which was sat a person of above-pensionable age. The staff were encouraging a singalong for which there was slow take-up. One or two of the residents were making strange, deeply personal noises, some of which appeared to convey pain or, worse, abject, bottomless misery.

If the people here had been looking for a distraction, then our arrival provided it. A collective attention fell upon us as I desperately scanned the room for its sole familiar face, but found only dozens of helpless eyes peering back at me in rheumy curiosity.

Suddenly, '*Neekolas!*', and a commotion in one corner, the bustle caused by a woman trying to force the one sitting directly in front of her out of the way so that she could get out and rush to me. My grandmother, and the only person to call me by my full name as my passport has it. It had been almost a year since I had seen her last – I had been ill, and unable to travel – and she had still been living in the flat then, alone, four years a widow and still making the slow adjustments. But now here was another far more seismic one: communal living. She looked pale and drawn, smaller than I remembered. I watched, uncomprehendingly at first, at the force she was employing to shove the woman in front of her out of the way. 'Muoveti!' she cried. *Move!*

Elena nudged me to do something, and I started, hurrying towards her, both in greeting but also to prevent a serious incident.

The other woman finally stood, leaving her chair vacant. 'Siediti,' my grandmother instructed me. *Sit.* And then, to the woman still standing in front of us, 'Via!' *Go!*

The sheer vehemence of her rudeness took me by surprise. The other woman stumbled away.

Our presence had now become the afternoon's entertainment. Nobody was singing any more, because everybody wanted to see what would happen next. My back to the crowd, I was aware of every pair of eyes resting heavily on me. I attempted to hug my grandmother, but she was agitated still, arms by her side, and so we stood awkwardly in front of one another, in front of our vacant chairs, actors in a play for which the next lines had yet to be written.

I was grateful, then, to the member of staff who intervened and suggested we repair to her room at the end of the corridor. Given something purposeful to do, she walked between Elena and me, holding an elbow each, and together we performed a slow foot shuffle in the lingering silence we left behind us. She held on tightly, knuckles white from the effort of her clench, her baby-blue eyes alive with a happiness that was to prove fleeting.

There were two beds in her room; she shared with somebody else. A woman was prostrate on the other bed by the window, still as a corpse but making a doleful melody with her open mouth.

'Mata,' my grandmother muttered, twirling a finger. *Mad*.

She commanded us to sit on her bed, which was made and neat and boasted hospital corners, while she made her way over to a cupboard. It was narrow, long and thin, like those found in schools, insufficient to needs. I realised quickly that it was hers, and that, worse, it contained what must be her few remaining possessions.

The rest of her things had gone now. When she had given up her flat a year before, the landlord had been keen to redecorate and put it on the market quickly. In a fit of anger at being, as she saw it, forced out of her home against her will, she had rashly consigned her worldly goods to charity – items of clothing and furniture, and keepsakes and mementos that dated back decades. The fury fuelled her still.

She came back from the cupboard holding a tin. The tin was familiar. For years it had contained boiled sweets, one or two of which my grand-father would permit us to suck nightly during a post-prandial game of cards. Any more than one or two was not allowed; too much sugar, bad for your teeth. The smell that drifted from the cupboard now, and the few clothes that hung there, was also strongly redolent of my past. Bronnley English Fern, a distinctively sharp perfume my mother had first brought back for them from London in 1965, a tradition I continued each time I visited, no matter how hard it became to track down.

She opened the tin and offered us sweets, as many as we liked because, she seemed to suggest from the mischievous look she gave, my grandfather was no longer around to interfere. From her bedside table, she brought out a packet of biscuits and, beneath these, several photograph albums. Still we hadn't talked, hadn't even said anything beyond a cursory hello. If we were still in her flat, she would have offered us food, a sandwich, some coffee, my usual boiled egg. But here she had no ready access to the kitchen; biscuits would have to do.

I wanted to ask her how she was, to hold her hand and remind her that I hadn't forgotten about her, and that I never would. I wanted to explain what deep down she already knew: that round-the-clock care had become imperative. She had needed someone to look after her, and this, we had decided, was our best, our *only*, option. I wanted to impress upon her, with all the diplomacy I could muster, that this relinquishing of life as she knew it was the price of having lived for so very long.

I said her name, Nonna, but she either didn't hear me or didn't want to. She was leafing through the photograph albums now, and pointing out pictures to Elena. We had seen them all before: me as a baby, a toddler, an ill-advisedly dressed teen.

But now, suddenly, the albums were discarded. The woman in the next bed had begun to moan louder, and the anger reached my grandmother in a rush. She hated it here, she told us. The staff! The food! Her bed! Her fellow inmates! She wanted her privacy back, her things, her life. Her eyes were blazing, and though she was still shrunken, she appeared huge, voluble. I was frightened by what I saw, because what I saw was how wretched things had become, and how helpless I was to alleviate her circumstances, her suffering.

We returned several times over the following days, and after seeking permission from staff on our last day, we left the compound together and wandered down the road to a café, she leaning heavily on my arm for support. We ordered coffee and croissants, and she was bewildered that the place was being run by Chinese people who somehow spoke to her in fluent Italian, further confirmation that the world, and even her neighbourhood, was moving forward without her.

And then it was time for us to leave. 'To London,' I told her, 'and the girls.'

She nodded once. She understood.

Back at the home, she accompanied us to the lift where we said our goodbyes and where we left everything else, all of it, pregnantly unsaid. She hugged me tight, the powdery white skin of her cheek so soft against my stubble. I tried not to cry as I told her that I would be back soon, and that I would bring the girls with me next time. I was not sure if she believed me, but then I was not sure if I believed it myself. Would there even be a next time?

I smiled at her, and she returned it in full, with the teeth I knew to be false. 'Si,' she said, clutching me close. *Yes.*

The lift arrived. She ushered us into it, then watched, her blue eyes swimming in unspilled tears as the doors closed, taking us down, back out to freedom and away from her.

On the way out, I bumped into a large man who recognised me before I did him. An old neighbour of my grandparents', a loud and boisterous man whose vigorous enthusiasm had always intimidated me into introversion. I used to cross the road to avoid him. I didn't, this time. We shook hands, and he pulled me into a garlic embrace.

'Eh, la Nonna,' he said to me, shaking his head with sadness but also, I thought, admiration at her staying power. 'La Nonna.'

How to acclimatise

A small Italian neighbourhood is not like your large unfriendly city. People expect you to be nice here, courteous, approachable; they expect conversation. So when accompanying your grandparent – invariably your grandmother – to the local shops, you can anticipate stopping to say hello to everyone you come into contact with, even if this necessitates crossing the busy road. If they don't catch your eye, you catch theirs. Wave. Say 'Ciao!' loudly, but not facetiously.

It may well be true that the baker is busy, as the queue stretching right out of the shop indicates, but be patient while your grandmother explains to her the obvious: that you have come for a visit, just a few days unfortunately, but better than nothing, that you have *come all the way from London, by aeroplane, that you are a father now, it was your birthday recently. And do offer up the obligatory compliments: that you love the baker's bread rolls, particularly the* michette vuote. *When the baker tells you that her cousin's grown-up children went to London three years ago and visited Harrods, simply smile and nod and repeat the word, 'Harrods'. This is all it takes to please her, and to please your grandmother, and it is not asking much, is it?*

. . . .

seven

At the very moment it seemed that losing her imminently was a distinct probability, I found myself wanting to get to know her again, but properly now. In her memoir, *A Life of My Own*, Claire Tomalin writes: 'People are spurred to write by the death of parents, as though they [feel] suddenly they must catch it now, before things fade too far into the distance.' My own mother had been dead for over a decade, and once my grandmother was gone, the door would close. If not now,

I thought, then never. I spoke to friends about the importance of their own relatives. Had they plundered their respective histories? Did they care enough to do so? Or did they, like me, toy with leaving it too late, these great repositories of untold stories forever unplundered, then lost?

We take for granted those things that are always around us, the people that are always there. There was drama in my family's past, ruptures between the generations that had wrenched them apart, and shameful secrets that kept them that way. I knew that these stories would fascinate me, compel me, so why had I not tried to find out about them sooner? Could I still find answers?

More and more people, it seemed, are looking for answers of their own. On a societal level, interest in our own personal genealogies is increasing. There are television programmes devoted to the tracing of family trees, and there are websites to help us navigate hidden histories. No more is it considered the sole pursuit of the recently retired, or the upper middle classes keen to have it confirmed that they are in fact descended from barons. More than a third of all Britons have now attempted to trace their ancestors online, and not simply because it is easier to do so than ever before. Perhaps because we live in a world that is becoming more diverse and increasingly fragmented, we know that we are losing something important, and that our sense of identity is evaporating. Personal histories are slippery things. Our own might mean precious little to us for great chunks of our lives, but at some point, they will.

At some point we will have questions for which we will crave answers.

It isn't easy to persuade young children that a trip to visit their aged relative in a care home constitutes a holiday, and so, on our annual visits to northern Italy to do just that, we attempt to ameliorate them by tacking on a few extra days afterwards to take in the nearby sights – and eat ice cream. In months like February and April, this means the lakes, the old towns of reachable cities, and, once, Venice in the middle of its festival. But when we went in July one year, we hired a car for the week and drove to the seaside resort of Portorož, just across the Italian border in Slovenia, my grandmother's place of birth.

I had reached that point in life where I no longer felt it necessary to avail myself of local history and culture, and was perfectly happy to lounge on the beach every day, reading. Which is what we did in Portorož, largely without complaint. But one day it rained heavily, with more forecast, so we decided

to drive somewhere. Requiring an endpoint, a destination, I thought it might be interesting to head
towards the tiny town in which my grandmother
had grown up, and which I had visited infrequently,
maybe no more than three or four times over the
previous four decades. I remember her house as old,
quaintly outdated even then, simple and basic, and,
apart from a new bathroom, entirely unmodernised,
the whole place heated by a furnace located in what
I seem to recall was the 'black kitchen' (black from
all the soot). Until the early 1980s, it didn't have an
indoor toilet, and the milk came from the next-door
neighbour's cow rather than the local shop, for the
simple reason that there wasn't one, the nearest being
a twenty-minute drive away. I once spent two weeks
there with my grandparents during a sweltering summer, surrounded by alpine splendour, endless rolling
hills and the dreadful absence of other teenagers. I
had never been so bored in all my life.

Now, we drove for a good couple of hours before finding signposts, and arrived to bright skies, and a town changed beyond all recognition. Where once there had been isolated houses dotted sporadically here and there, there were now many more, all of them modern and smart, with paved driveways and, in place of the tractors I remember, smart German saloon cars. There were shops, a supermarket. We followed the road that led into the hills where the house had been, but I recognised nothing. It was Elena who spotted it first, despite having only ever seen it in photographs. We stopped abruptly in the middle of the eerily empty road. At first it was difficult to believe what we were seeing. The house was precisely as I remembered it, in its own field, painted freshly white under a thatched, sloping roof. It looked untouched, as if forgotten, yet clearly preserved. We parked on a dirt track, then walked through high grass towards it, the unexpected sun hot on our backs.

'We could have stayed at the beach,' Amaya noted.

Peering through the windows was like witnessing a three-dimensional unfolding of my memory: the same sparse furniture arranged in the same spartan way, the same wooden chairs, the same trinkets on the mantelpiece. It reminded me now, as it did years ago, of *The Waltons*, of *Little House on the Prairie* – of how people used to live before they invented carpets, wallpaper, television.

At approximately the same time that Evie pointed out an elderly man in elderly clothing walking across the field towards us, Elena drew our attention to a blue plaque affixed to the outside wall, commemorating the fact that the house, designed by my grandmother's cousin, a famed local architect who was subsequently interred in a concentration camp during the Second World War, was now a site of historical importance, the perfect example of the kind of houses that were made in this region a century previously.

This place, then, was a living museum, and I had had no idea.

The elderly man was upon us now, smiling in welcome to reveal teeth that hadn't seen a dentist in decades. I asked him, in Italian, if he spoke Italian. He answered me, in Slovenian, that he didn't. English? I wondered. Helpfully trying to meet me halfway, he offered instead: 'Deutsche?' We ultimately made do with semaphore, and the raised voices people with no lingua franca invariably employ when no other option presents itself, and from this he was able to discern who I was, and my relation to this place. I mentioned my mother's name, Natasha, and he broke out into a smile. From the front pocket of his dungarees he produced a large iron key, the key to the front door. By now we were all rapt with anticipation, this previously aimless day out suddenly taking on a historical significance I kidded myself my children might remember in years to come.

We stepped over the threshold and, for me, into a heady sense of the past, snapshots swimming up of my previous visits in 1977, 1984 and in 1990 when I came here with a girlfriend. We had been hosted, that time, by the kindly family next door, where for dinner they fed us deep bowls of clear broth with a dirty great silvery fish bobbing gently in it. 'Eat!' they encouraged.

The house was dark and smelled of its age, but was impossibly beautiful in its antique simplicity and rustic, woodloused charm. The man showed us into the living room, and I explained to the girls that the huge wrought-iron stove that dominated almost a quarter of the floor was the house's heating system: feed the furnace in the black kitchen, and the front room radiates its warmth. From a small cupboard on the wall, the man produced a bottle of grappa, and toasted our good health.

I was talking rapidly to the girls now, reliving my memories here, hoping perhaps in vain to further pique their interest. In Elena Ferrante's 2006 novel *The Lost Daughter*, she writes: 'How foolish to think you can tell your children about yourself before they're at least fifty. To ask to be seen by them as a person and not a function. To say: I am your history, you begin from me, listen to me, it could be useful to you.' My daughters' attention spans were as limited as mine had been at their ages, but nevertheless they did seem intrigued. In the car afterwards, Evie began asking questions to which I found I didn't know the answer. Again I was reminded of all that I didn't know, and that soon I would lose the chance forever. The dead take their secrets with them.

Don't they?

A few years ago, I passed the night with friends around a Ouija board. Wine had been drunk beforehand. We spent several bewildering hours suspending disbelief while the planchette swung with gusto around the board's alphabet, assiduously spelling out messages for us. It seemed that we could request an audience with some of our dearly departed just as efficiently as if we had called them on the phone, and each in turn appeared only too eager to communicate with us, one letter at a time. We spoke, often at length, with a dead aunt, a dead grandparent, and their responses were loquacious, melancholic, optimistic and even funny. None of us had any idea what was happening, or how, but it was riveting. After some time, it was my turn to commune. I called up my mother and, lo, my mother 'arrived', if that's the word I'm looking for here. Following my friends' lead, I asked her if there was anything she wanted to tell me, and I braced myself for her answer, tingling with anticipation at what she might wish to convey to me from beyond the grave out there in the ether.

'N' was the first letter the planchette alighted on. We said it out loud to register to the spirit that we were following its lead, and awaiting more. 'O' was the second.

No.

It took me three years to start seeking answers to those questions, and I did it this time with one of the living. To coincide with another of our visits to the care home, I made contact with Loretta, an old friend of my mother's in Milan, and asked if we could meet. I told her why. She went quiet on the phone before agreeing. 'Of course,' she said. 'See you soon.'

When I arrived at her small, orderly flat in the heart of the city, I found that she wasn't alone. On the living-room floor, surrounded by blocks of Lego, sat her grandson, half Italian, half Bulgarian and, right now, full of flu. 'He couldn't go to school today,' she explained. 'I'm sorry.' He was six years old, and distinctly not happy to see me. Loretta, who retired several years ago, provides daily care for her two grandchildren while her son and daughter-in-law work. I asked if she likes it.

'Yes, naturally,' she said, adding, 'because, you see, otherwise I am alone.'

I have known Loretta for most of my life, and have always liked her. While other Italians of my grandparents' acquaintance were large and boisterous, and fond, in that Italian way, of pinching a child's cheek with the forefinger and thumb instead of simply saying hello like normal people, Loretta was cool and chic and slightly aloof, as if designed by Yves Saint Laurent, and dressed by Chanel. She was softly spoken, and spoke perfect English. She was once someone important in an import/export electronics firm, and had her own office. I remember us going to see her in it, the luxury of its thick carpet, its leather-backed chairs. For a present one time, she gave me a Walkman, the first of its kind I had seen. I treasured it.

It had been four years since I saw her last. She is the close family friend I referred to earlier, the one who had been like a daughter to my grandparents and who helped oversee my grandmother's move into the care home. They haven't seen one another since, my grandmother still convinced that Loretta is to blame for her loss of independence when it is clear, to me, that she is anything but. She was seventy-four now, the age my mother would have been were she still alive. The small talk I had anticipated doesn't happen. Her grandchild, snotty and surly, was complaining loudly, and flatly refused the offer of lunch until a phone call to his mother persuaded him otherwise. Afterwards, he settled in the kitchen in front of the television while we sat in the next room. I took out my dictaphone to record our conversation, but while in one sense it felt just like another interview for me, the answers she gave me made it unlike any I had ever previously conducted.

Loretta to me seemed hesitant, almost reluctant to talk, as if by my asking her to rake over my family history, I was asking her to rake over a part of hers, too. And who was I to do that? We sat in silence for what to me proved several awkward moments as she stared deeply into the patterned tablecloth. From the kitchen, the sounds of cartoons entertaining her grandchild drifted in like cigarette smoke, and my impulse was to wave them away, to have

Loretta stay focused only on me, and the story, and to keep telling it.

She apologised for her English, telling me that she hasn't spoken it properly in years, but she still seemed perfectly fluent, and I pointed out the obvious: that she is far better in my language than I am in hers. Then she began.

It was at some point during the Second World War, she told me, that my grandmother arrived in Italy from Yugoslavia. She was with her boyfriend, not an Italian, but a Russian. They had been in a relationship for at least a year, and were happy. I wanted more details. How easy would it have been for two people whose countries were at war to be in a relationship for that long, much less in a contented one? Was he a soldier, and what was her part in the war effort? Loretta admitted that she didn't know.

Later, I asked a historian for a few pointers. It's confusing, he told me, a puzzle. The boyfriend might have been Russian, or actually Soviet, and if Soviet, was he Ukrainian, or some other member of the USSR? By 1943, Yugoslavia was ostensibly occupied by Italian troops until that September, when they opted out of the war. The whole place, he said, was a mess. My real grandfather could have been fighting for the Germans voluntarily, because lots did, or he could have been drafted into the German army and then escaped. If he was in Yugoslavia, where Loretta says he first met my grandmother, he was probably there with a German unit. If he was a communist, he might have followed Yugoslavia's leader, Tito, or he might have fled into Italy and joined the Partisans.

Early that year, my grandmother discovered that she was pregnant (my mother was born that Christmas Eve). Falling pregnant out of wedlock in a Catholic country was highly inadvisable in those times. My grandmother wanted quickly to remedy the situation, Loretta relayed, and suggested to her Russian boyfriend that they get married. But he wasn't interested in marriage. He told her he was happy that they continue as they were.

'So she left him. She broke off their relationship, and never saw him again.'

Loretta doesn't know his name, and so he, my real grandfather, was as gone from my life as quickly as he had arrived, a mystery I am not about to solve any time soon. But he is Russian, not Italian. And so I am a quarter Russian. This fact, as new as a new penny, unsettles me in a way I hadn't anticipated, and I'm not entirely sure why.

Russian? Христос!

At that point, Loretta explained, my grandfather was still living at home in Milan with his mother. Until recently, his brother had been living with them, and whether he was older or younger, she didn't know.

I had always assumed him to have been an only child, because I never saw evidence to the contrary. Their home was a small flat in the centre of the city, so small that the brothers, even in adulthood, had been required to share a bed.

Loretta trailed off at this point, and didn't look at me. Eventually, she started speaking again. 'I don't know whether to tell you this, but . . .' She faltered. Gently, I encouraged her to please tell me. It didn't matter how bad it was. It's family; I wanted to know. She continued.

One morning, my grandfather woke up to find that his brother, beside him, was dead. Suicide. He would never speak of this to anyone, and my grandmother had only told Loretta a few short years ago. I asked how he had killed himself. 'I don't know, she never said. But she did say that the bed was covered with blood, and that he, your grandfather, was very shocked. Very.'

I try to see him now in a new light, in lingering shock and trauma, the kind that never fully diminishes, that throws shadows on everything that follows. Perhaps, then, he saw my grandmother and her daughter as solace for his unhappy life, a ready-made family within which he could reinvent himself and attain a kind of – what? Normality? Perhaps, yes. But his own mother was less taken by the idea. She told him that she didn't approve of his new wife, and certainly not the illegitimate daughter. After the wedding, which I can only imagine was a small, scant affair, they were required to move in with her, but his mother soon made it clear that there was no place in her house for the girl, the bastard, my mother.

'So she gave her up,' Loretta said.

'Who?' I asked, unclear, not certain what she meant.

'Your grandmother. She sent her to a convent.'

'For how long?'

'I don't know. Several years? And it was for this reason that your mother never forgave her: that she could give her up, just like that. She never accepted the fact that your grandmother got married and didn't take her with her. And she never forgot it.'

This was all news to me. But was it? Was it really? I hate to think that my mother had told me all of this at some point during my childhood but that I blithely forgot it because it wasn't particularly important to me then. I knew about the convent, but I'd thought that she had attended a convent as a teenager in much the same way a child would a boarding school. She had been in her teens, I thought. But, Loretta said now, 'She was younger, four or maybe five.'

Her mother and new stepfather did visit, and frequently, and at some point she was permitted to come back home. I have photographs of them all together, my grandfather's mother a stout, squarish woman dressed in widow's black, and possessed of a face made for scowling. But, Loretta said, 'She was not happy at home. There was always . . . tension. By the time I met her, she wanted to go to England, to leave her family, and to not come back.'

Loretta met my mother when they were both at school studying English. They were eighteen. Two years later, in 1963, my mother flew to London. She worked first as a nanny, then held an office job at the Italian Domestic Agency. She lived in Finchley, then on the Earls Court Road. Six months later, Loretta joined her. It was an exciting time to be in the city. London was just getting swinging. The Beatles were happening. These two young friends were now sharing a flat with several other Italian women. They were free, and single, and had disposable incomes.

I asked Loretta what life was like for my mother, at last far from the constraints of her parents. Did she savour her freedom, enjoy herself?

Her answer came with a frown. 'I don't know. Your mother was always so . . . so serious. She was reflective; depressive I would say. She was always trying to be perfect, and never to do anything wrong. She over-thought a lot, and I don't think she was an easy person. We were a group of girls, a group of Italians, but the only one who could really get on with her was me.'

I was inexpressibly sad to hear this, and felt a lump rising in my throat.

'She was, I don't know . . . too straight, perhaps. She didn't allow herself to have fun. And she didn't do the things that maybe one would do when you are free in London at that age. I felt that she always had on her shoulders some kind of responsibility, to do right, to be good.' A shake of the head. 'I don't know.'

There was, for a time, some relief, some shedding of responsibility in pursuit of fun. Shortly after arriving in London, she met an Italian man, Mimmo. Loretta's expression lifted when she spoke of him. 'Mimmo was a special person, so open, always laughing and happy, a person like that.' Though they were very different characters, he and my mother fell in love. He proposed quickly, and she accepted. He wrote a letter to my grandparents asking for her hand in marriage, and posted it the day he arrived back in Italy to visit his own family. Later that same afternoon, he went for a swim in the local river. Mimmo had been a strong swimmer, and by all accounts could have competed nationally. But on that afternoon the river's current was too strong. He was swept along, carried away and under. He drowned.

News hadn't reached them by the following morning, when my grandparents received his written request. They felt unambiguous delight: their daughter, and her fiancé, would be coming back to Italy, to live, to be near them again.

'Your mother took his death very hard,' Loretta said. 'Very hard.'

She returned for the funeral. Her parents urged her to stay on, but she went back to London as soon as she could. Within a year she had met my father, a Yorkshireman who had relocated to the capital to work, initially, in the hotel business. Their romance progressed quickly. My mother telephoned home to say that she was getting married.

'They were not happy with this,' she said. 'They flew to London to convince her to come back with them. They couldn't accept that their girl was going to live so far away. But she didn't care, she just sent them home.'

They were never much taken with my father. Following my birth, we moved into our tower block where we would frequently be burgled and where, on occasion, distraught people would take our lift up to the nineteenth floor, ten floors above us, and throw themselves off the roof. There were perhaps better places to grow up. My father, by now working in the travel industry, was away a lot, and my grandparents worried for my mother. They didn't like where we were living, *how* we were living. They didn't like my father. 'The marriage won't last,' they taunted. 'It will end in tears.' When it eventually did, a decade later, they insisted once again that she return to Milan. And once again she resisted.

'Your mother was very strong but very stubborn, just like your grandmother, in fact,' Loretta said. 'Both women, they always said what they felt. I know that your grandmother felt guilty for putting her in the convent that time, but she had apologised, she wanted to move on, to forget. But your mother, she never could.'

I breathed deeply, amazed by the drama of it all, so much of which I never knew. I did recall my mother asking whether I might like to move to Milan, because there, she promised, we would have more support than we did in London. The schools were good, she said. And teenagers there were legally permitted to have a moped at the age of fourteen. I was tempted by the prospect of a Vespa and the associated prospect, however distant, of an actual Italian girlfriend, but I resisted. I didn't want to leave London, home, my friends. My mother never put up much fight because she didn't want to move to Italy any more than I did.

I think of her, and remember her, as an amazing woman – strong-willed, independent, a feminist – but a contradictory one also. For me she was always there and always supportive, and she was appealingly weird in a way I would only come to appreciate much later: certainly the only yoga enthusiast in Peckham in the 1970s, and probably the only vegetarian, too. She was extolling the virtues of acidophilus and Echinacea to me a good three decades before I came to see their benefits for myself.

But throughout life she was hampered by depression and unhappiness. There were secretive bouts of anorexia and bulimia; I would hear her vomiting in the bathroom behind a closed door, but when I tried to discuss it with her, she snapped at me and changed the subject. When I heard her again, I'd tiptoe down the stairs and into the living room, where I turned the sound up loud on the television. Her marriage ending must have broken whatever spirit she had left after such a difficult childhood, and though she could be such wonderful company – she loved films, loved books, loved talking – she was lonely and unfulfilled, forever searching for something that would continue to elude her. She was angry a lot, rarely at me, always at herself and her inability to break her often self-destructive cycles.

When she became ill with pancreatic cancer at the beginning of 1999, the doctors gave her six months. She lasted eleven. Her reaction to it was, to me, slightly deranged. Pancreatic cancer is painful. There is no scale of 1 to 10, because it's more, always more. At first she took painkillers, but increasingly chose not to. Instead, she appeared to accept it, believing that she had developed it because of stress brought on by long-term discontent. She felt she had failed at life, and that this was her ultimate punishment. She would endure it because she deserved it – fate, kismet, karma.

At this point, I was living at the other end of London from her. For many of those eleven cancerous months, my nightly meal was a sandwich on the Northern line as I travelled to visit her. Sometimes she was communicative and happy; mostly, she was not. She needed someone to direct her anger at, and I was the only one there. I watched, front row, as the cancer did its highly efficient work and transformed her from a woman who, late in life, had found some purpose and contentment – she had left her job to focus entirely on her pursuit in Tai Chi, and the meditative calm it offered – to a scooped-out husk who had been all but worn away by pain, and driven half mad because of it. I pleaded with her relentlessly: take the morphine, toss the St John's wort away, allow the doctors to help. But every week I watched her deplete. There was cruelty in this.

Throughout that time, my grandparents chose not to visit. I don't remember questioning their decision so much as blindly accepting it. They hadn't come to London for many years anyway, and had always hated travelling too far from home. My grandfather had his routines, and my grandmother had for so long played the loyal wife that this role trumped the secondary maternal one.

There was only one point during my conversation with Loretta that she fully raised her voice, and it came now, during the subject of my mother's illness.

'You know,' she said, 'I have never forgiven your grandmother for not making the decision to go and visit her. I kept telling her that she should go, that if your grandfather didn't want to go with her, he would be fine at home alone. And even if not, then to hell with him! Her daughter was ill! She needed to be with her.'

She only conceded when Loretta herself decided to fly over, at which point my grandmother quickly agreed to accompany her. A neighbour would look in on my grandfather at mealtimes. They came for just two days in October, heading straight from the airport to the hospice where my mother was curled up skeletal on a bed that had, over the previous weeks, become far too big for her. I had been encouraged by the prospect of their arrival, and was full of hope, but my mother's response was hers alone, and nothing if not consistent. She didn't want to see them, didn't want to talk. There was no mellowing at this late, final stage. My mother refused even to feign civility; she merely appraised them in a taunting silence while I looked into her eyes to see if I could unravel what lay behind them. I stood by my grandmother's side, and I watched as the pain etched itself into her, her expression so full of pleading. I felt for her. I willed my mother to make an effort, to make amends in the short time they had left.

Loretta and I retreated, to give them privacy, sitting in a corridor and largely failing to make small talk. My grandmother re-emerged an hour later, tears streaming down her face. My suggestion of a late dinner somewhere was politely declined.

'They fought,' Loretta told me now. 'When we got back to the hotel, your grandmother was crying nearly all the night, but she wouldn't tell me why, what their fight had been about. She wouldn't tell me anything.'

It seems that this is not in any way untypical of families with their buried secrets and festering resentments. We've all got them, and not all wounds heal. I had always been aware that there had been some lingering poison existing there, but never the extent of it, never the full reasons why. All I'd known is that I had been spared the brunt of it, and that my own relationship with my mother's mother was so very different from hers. This was her issue, her grudge, not mine. To me, my grandmother had only ever been kindly, doting and benevolent. She'd behaved towards her daughter the way she had behaved, and for what I presume was good reason, or perhaps out of desperation, and it is a shame that my mother couldn't accept this, and over time learn to sympathise and empathise. She could have chosen to forgive her, to see things from her perspective: a beleaguered single mother in a devoutly Catholic country where codes of conduct were being forcefully reasserted after the years of chaos that come with war.

But she didn't.

My mother died a month after their visit, on November 27, the occasion of my grandmother's eighty-first birthday. They didn't attend the funeral. Every year thereafter, when I called her to wish her a happy birthday, she said my mother's name to me, voicing it aloud for no other reason than she had to, a maternal compulsion, and then burst once again into copious tears that extinguished any semblance of celebration, and rendered all further conversation irrelevant.

What else was there to say?

How to remember us

Before you go, I want to give you something to remember us by. It's clear to me you need some clothes, because why else would you have worn the same pair of jeans all week, with the rips at the knees? You really should have let me fix them for you. It wouldn't have been any trouble. Anyway, your grandfather has many trousers here, and he doesn't wear most of them. Look at these ones. Corduroys! And brown is always fashionable. No matter if they are too long and too wide, I can take them up, and in. Try them on, let me see you in them.

For consecutive birthdays, we will buy you a wallet made from real Italian leather. You may well let them pile up in a drawer at home, each unused and still in their presentation boxes, but eventually you will use *every one of them. Life is long. You will always need to keep your money somewhere.*

Here, take these cups. They are made from china. For coffee. Every time you have your morning espresso, think of us. No, no. I will wrap them up so they won't break in your luggage. You can have the saucers, too. Do you have spoons in London?

For your wife, this scarf. A coat, perhaps? The collar is real fur. Or these lace doilies, beautiful for decoration. This umbrella? For the plane, some sandwiches. Four, so you won't go hungry. Ham, cheese, tomatoes. And for the fridge at home: tortellini, ravioli. Gnocchi. Do you know gnocchi? You do? Some sweets for the plane, so your ears won't pop.

Take the sweets. Remember us, yes? Don't forget.

. . . .

eight

My grandmother managed to last just six months in her first care home, a long enough acclimatisation period perhaps, but one in which she failed to settle. Her anger required a breaking point to usher in significant change, and this came when she received an unexpected visit from old friends she hadn't seen in years. They were two sisters whose parents had been neighbours decades before. Revisiting the area, they tracked her down to the facility and were so

upset by the levels of her distress that they promised to help. Within days, they suggested we could
transfer her to an alternative home closer to where
they lived, an hour north of Milan. This way, they
said, she would have the infrastructure of what she
needed most: a family nearby, even if they weren't
really family at all. Whenever I came to visit, they
promised, I could stay with them. *La mia casa è la
tua casa.* They would handle all the paperwork and
bureaucracy that required the transfer from one
institution to another, and they could even help
manage her finances.

I admired the gesture, and could find no comparison for their generosity. People really behave like
this, I wondered? So selflessly? However, I couldn't
help but doubt the veracity of their undeniably well-
intentioned offer. These were busy people already,
both in their fifties, with grown and still-growing
children, high-pressure jobs and, though I didn't

know it yet, illness to deal with. Where would my grandmother fit in all this?

But they were insistent, preposterously keen even, convinced it was a good idea, the only viable one in the circumstances. My grandmother could be their guest every Sunday at big family lunches, and one of the sisters, Lucilla, would visit her each afternoon after work. 'It's on my way,' she insisted.

When I told friends of this amazing act of kindness, some advised caution. Perhaps they were after my grandmother's money, they suggested. My grandmother had no money, and no possessions of any discernible value. But the elderly are vulnerable in all sorts of ways, and so I remained wary, a pessimism born out of exposure to scaremongering headlines and television documentaries. Nevertheless, to my grandmother's very great relief, the move was swiftly arranged, she felt immediately more settled and accepting of her surroundings, and for the next couple of years she did indeed become part of this bustling, extended family. They even successfully filed for years' worth of unclaimed benefits on her behalf, making her more financially independent than she had been in a long time. And when Lucilla's mother moved into the care home herself, she had a proper friend with her, albeit one she grew jealous of during family visits, both women craving the lion's share of their attention. This must have divided Lucilla's loyalties, and tested her patience, but by now Lucilla had revealed herself to me as a living saint, someone who had seen how cruel life could become for those that lived it long enough and wanted only to ameliorate their suffering. When she died, cruelly, after a brief illness in 2016, my grandmother was utterly bereft. A few months later, we went to pay our respects at Lucilla's grave, and she gripped onto me with a sadness that did dreadful things to her face, rearranging it into a grimace of pain so vividly articulated I felt it like a slap. But these feelings she bore. By the age of ninety-six, my grandmother had become an expert in the industry of death.

She is ninety-eight as I write these words, very nearly ninety-nine. We saw her just a few short months ago, our annual pilgrimage via easyJet, an airline whose frequent-flyer programme I keep meaning to sign up to, and keep forgetting. She is wearing her age now far more plainly, largely deaf and completely toothless (she no longer wears the dentures due to gum erosion), and is sufficiently unstable on her legs to require wheels to get around. Bronchitis had laid her low the previous autumn, but not as low as doctors had predicted. She improved.

It is February when we visit, a Wednesday. Wednesday in this tiny town is market day, and so we wrap her up in successive layers until she is as coddled as a newborn, and we wheel her out of the compound for the first time in six months.

This is a place where you don't meet many pedestrians, but today it is packed, people clustered around a hodgepodge of stalls selling clothes and underwear, more underwear than seems strictly necessary for a place this size, girdles and Playtex bras dangling from countless hooks, alongside meat vans selling whole roast chickens and, towards the end of the street, a pet area that hawks miniature hamsters, nervous goldfish, imprisoned parakeets. It is warm in the sunshine, and brisk in the shade as we stop to buy sweets for the girls. Rita, an old friend of Lucilla's who now attends to my grandmother on most days, insists on buying my daughters several kilos' worth of technicoloured chews while my grandmother watches on with an unreadable look on her face.

There is no real conversation to be had. She can't

hear what I'm saying, can't make out my hopelessly faltering efforts, and so we simply smile at each other a lot, and occasionally nod as if to say: look, here we are, together again. Prompted by a maternal concern that won't die until she does, she asks inter-mittently whether I am cold, whether the girls are cold. She no longer asks about the frequency of my bowel movements as she once did, but my optimum health remains at the forefront of her diminishing mind. What she says most is, 'Sei contento?' *Are you happy?* That is all she really wants to know, and it's imperative for her that I am, that we all are.

'Yes,' I tell her. 'Yes we are.'

I know that she is often upset and distressed, still pining for the life she lost, and that sometimes she is angry, refusing to eat, refusing to go to bed when they tell her, refusing to swallow the pills that so many of her fellow inmates are given here to keep them quiet and untroublesome. Does she feel that

I have abandoned her at this critical time in her life? Does she continue to register her daughter's absence? If her daughter was still here, then things would have been different. They might not have been any better, but they would have been different.

'Her moods change a lot,' Rita tells me sadly. 'It's her age.'

But today, at least for now, she seems happy, and I hold on to this.

We stand alongside the sweet stall, and I look down at her, and smile. Her eyes remain a pure translucent blue, and if the rest of her is merely obeying the laws of nature by losing definition and steadily closing down, then it is her eyes alone that manage to convey a continued vivacity to counter-act her vintage. They sparkle in the sunshine, and in them I see the very history of her life and times, her disappointments and mistakes, her secrets and torments, delights and satisfactions. There is nothing more now I can tell her, and nothing she can tell me. We've known each other for almost half a century, two intimately connected strangers who only ever managed to present to one another edited versions of themselves. For me, this is all I have ever known and so it has been enough. The bond endures.

When we are ready to leave for what may, this time, just like the last time, be the final time, Rita wheels her down to the gate so that she can watch us get into our hire car and drive off. We wave but she doesn't, perhaps because she no longer can. I wonder how aware she still is, and whether she knows that I love her, that we all love her, that even though they don't show it, her great-granddaughters will surely remember these moments and tell their own great-granddaughters about her one day, which means that she will live on as departed family members always have, always do and always will.

I hope she knows.

Acknowledgements

Mostly, I would like to thank Jennie Condell for giving me the opportunity in the first place, and to her, Pippa Crane, and everyone at Elliott & Thompson for their advice, guidance and saintly patience. In the last few years, several incredibly selfless women have been there to help my grandmother, and to make her life more bearable. Loretta, Lucilla, Paola and Rita – Elena, too – I am eternally grateful to each of you. And to Amaya and Evie: if either of you ever make me a grandfather one day – not soon, but years and years into the future, *years* – be nice to me, yes?